Mission to the Volga

Letter from the General Editor

The Library of Arabic Literature series offers Arabic editions and English translations of significant works of Arabic literature, with an emphasis on the seventh to nineteenth centuries. The Library of Arabic Literature thus includes texts from the pre-Islamic era to the

LIBRARY OF
المكتبة
ARABIC
العربية
LITERATURE

cusp of the modern period, and encompasses a wide range of genres, including poetry, poetics, fiction, religion, philosophy, law, science, history, and historiography.

Books in the series are edited and translated by internationally recognized scholars and are published in parallel-text format with Arabic and English on facing pages, and are also made available as English-only paperbacks.

The Library encourages scholars to produce authoritative, though not necessarily critical, Arabic editions, accompanied by modern, lucid English translations. Its ultimate goal is to introduce the rich, largely untapped Arabic literary heritage to both a general audience of readers as well as to scholars and students.

The Library of Arabic Literature is supported by a grant from the New York University Abu Dhabi Institute and is published by NYU Press.

Philip F. Kennedy

General Editor, Library of Arabic Literature

About this Paperback

This paperback edition differs in a few respects from its dual-language hardcover predecessor. Because of the compact trim size the pagination has changed, but paragraph numbering has been retained to facilitate cross-referencing with the hardcover. Material that referred to the Arabic edition has been updated to reflect the English-only format, and other material has been corrected and updated where appropriate. For information about the Arabic edition on which this English translation is based and about how the LAL Arabic text was established, readers are referred to the hardcover.

Mission to the Volga

by

Aḥmad ibn Faḍlān

translated by
James E. Montgomery

foreword by
Tim Severin

volume editor
Shawkat M. Toorawa

New York University Press
New York

NEW YORK UNIVERSITY PRESS
New York

Library of Congress Cataloging-in-Publication Data
Names: Ibn Fadlan, Ahmad, active 922 author. | Montgomery, James E. (James Edward), 1962– translator. | Toorawa, Shawkat M. editor. | Severin, Timothy author of foreword.
Title: Mission to the Volga / by Ahmad ibn Fadlan ; translated by James E. Montgomery ; foreword by Tim Severin ; volume editor, Shawkat M. Toorawa.
Other titles: Kitab al-Rihlah ila malik al-Saqalibah. English
Description: New York : New York University Press, 2017. | Includes bibliographical references and index.
Identifiers: LCCN 2016038305 | ISBN 9781479899890 (pb : alk. paper) | ISBN 9781479826698 (e-book) | ISBN 9781479829750 (e-book)
Subjects: LCSH: Tatarstan (Russia)—Description and travel. | Bulgars (Turkic people)—Russia (Federation)—Volga River Region—History. | Ibn Fadlan, Ahmad, active 922—Travel—Asia, Central. | Volga River Region (Russia)—History.
Classification: LCC DK511.T17 I2313 2017 | DDC 914.7/45042—dc23
LC record available at https://lccn.loc.gov/2016038305

New York University Press books are printed on acid-free paper, and their binding materials are chosen for strength and durability.

Series design and composition by Nicole Hayward
Typeset in Adobe Text

Manufactured in the United States of America

10 9 8 7 6 5 4 3 2 1

For Josh, for the journey

Contents

Foreword

TIM SEVERIN

I was still a university student the only time I rode with a camel caravan. A gang of Baluch tribesmen were smuggling contraband to Hormuz on the shores of the Persian Gulf and had chosen to take an obscure track through highland wilderness to avoid police checkpoints. Marco Polo was likely to have used the same trail on his way to Cathay—I was trying to retrace his path using his description of the terrain—and the caravan was very small, some twenty beasts. The Baluch walked, leading the animals, but I had a broken foot so was permitted to perch up on an extremely uncomfortable saddle. I travelled with them for only a few days, but the memory of the discomfort is enough for me to appreciate what Ibn Faḍlān must have endured as he accompanied the mission to the Volga. Also I shared his sense of unease about the rapacity of his companions of the road.

In his tale, Ibn Faḍlān comes across as someone trying to make the best of a disagreeable but unavoidable situation. You sense his alarm when the citizens of al-Jurjāniyyah, the last city in Khwārazm before he enters the realm of the semi-nomadic Turks, warn him that extreme cold will make the next stage of his journey thoroughly unpleasant. They predict that he will perish unless he is warmly dressed, and one suspects they succeeded in persuading him to purchase the necessary extra garments from them.

While Ibn Faḍlān and his companions wait in al-Jurjāniyyah for the weather to improve, the mission purchases "Turkish" camels.

Were these animals locally bred and owned and therefore better able to cope with the harsh conditions that lay ahead? Or are we to infer that his idea of a "Turkish" camel is a two-humped Bactrian in contrast to the one-humped dromedary? Having arrived from Baghdad, Ibn Faḍlān would have been familiar with dromedaries, and they would have been better suited for the earlier stages of his journey as when skirting around the Dasht-e-Kavir. Beyond al-Jurjāniyyah, the Bactrians were certainly to be preferred.

What is clear is that al-Jurjāniyyah had a large livestock market to supply the needs of travellers. Our traveller mentions later that his caravan numbered three thousand mounts, though this included horses. Of this multitude, by no means all would have been pack animals carrying trade goods. Some camels, like Ibn Faḍlān's own mount, were for riding, and many would have been needed to carry the essential marching supplies. The camelmen were professionals: they knew from experience that the caravan would have to be self-sufficient on its journey, and for how long. So they packed sufficient bread, millet and cured meat to last three months. All this food would have to be loaded, together with tents, cooking gear, spare harnesses, fodder, and—significantly—equipment for crossing rivers. Here again one senses Ibn Faḍlān's puzzlement, then increasing concern, as he watches the camelmen spread camel hides flat on the ground, place the wooden frames of the camel saddles on top, then stretch the skins up and around the saddle frames. They are assembling and testing the rudimentary coracles that they will deploy when the caravan reaches the banks of the great rivers. The animals will be swum across, with much shouting and cajoling. Meanwhile small groups of travellers must balance in these makeshift vessels and paddle themselves and their goods to the far bank. Unsurprisingly, these make-do watercrafts prove to be none too stable and at least one capsizes during a river crossing, and the passengers drown.

So Ibn Faḍlān sets out from al-Jurjāniyyah under no illusions about whether that the road ahead is gruelling. It has neither bridges, fords, nor ferries and certainly no caravanserais to offer food and shelter. His worst fears are quickly realized. Two days out from al-Jurjāniyyah he finds himself perched on the back of a camel plodding through knee-deep snow. He is swaddled in so many layers of clothes that he can scarcely move, yet he is chilled to the bone. He feels he is ready to die. Plaintively he complains in one of his well-turned phrases, "It made the cold of Khwārazm seem like summer time."

Did Ibn Faḍlān take and keep notes as the caravan moved across the countryside at a modest average of ten miles per day? It is unlikely. Writing while on camel back is nigh-on impossible, and he would have been too wet, cold and woebegone at each campsite to do so. Also, there was little about the countryside that would have caught his eye. The terrain he crossed was largely featureless, flat and desolate, covered in snow at the outset, and scrubby grassland after the snowmelt. It remains as much a blank in his narrative as in the report written by the Franciscan friar Giovanni da Pian del Carpini who also rode to the Volga three centuries later as a papal legate to the Mongols.

We get to know more about Ibn Faḍlān when he encounters the semi-nomadic Turkish tribes. He is manifestly not a country man. He concludes that the sheep of the Turks were fat in the winter because they ate snow, only to lose condition in summer because they ate grass. Apparently he was unaware that in spring the flocks were shorn of their wool and so looked thinner. Coming from the splendid metropolis of Baghdad with its brick-built houses and convenient network of water channels, he is aghast at the habits of those who dwell in portable homes and regard water as a resource too precious to be used for personal hygiene. He portrays the Turks as uncouth, dirty and ignorant.

This honest assessment adds to the value of Ibn Faḍlān's narrative. He has no reason to be polite. We don't know for whom he compiled his account of his journey, but it is safe to say that he did not imagine that his audience would include Turkish tribesmen from the steppe who would take offense. Ibn Faḍlān was free to express his views, while also enhancing the self-regard of his Arab audience. He is a city sophisticate jotting down a selection of his most lively memories. It gives a freshness to his observations and he can express himself with style. In his account, for example, the burly ruler of the Bulghārs has a threatening voice that seems to come "from inside a barrel."

Sometimes one feels a little sorry for our traveller. His piety is offended when the camp muezzin mangles the correct call to prayer, and he shouts at the man to stop. He finds the food distasteful. Some has been stored in underground pits until it rots and smells. Then it is cooked in fish oil rather than the olive or vegetable oil to which he is accustomed. The result is greasy and unpalatable. Nor is he ever quite sure of his standing with his hosts. They can be suspicious and accommodating by turns, and occasionally downright hostile. Ibn Faḍlān admits he was "dazed and in a state of terror" after an interview with the Bulghār ruler who threw Ibn Faḍlān's official letters back at him, and demanded to know why he hadn't brought the money promised by Baghdad.

Yet Ibn Faḍlān doesn't give up. He does his best to ingratiate himself, handing out gifts of cloth, food, and spices that reflect the importance of the recipient. The leader of a less important tribe gets a not very expensive caftan, some flat bread, a handful of raisins and a hundred nuts, while the ruler of the Bulghārs receives a horse with a special saddle, medical ointment, clothes and pearls with a robe of honor for his wife.

There's an occasional hint that the Turks have been sizing him up and are making fun of him. A Turkish soldier picks a louse out of his clothing, kills it by cracking it with a fingernail, and licks it. He notices that Ibn Faḍlān is watching, so holds it up and says "Yum!" Surely it's a tease. So too when a Turk riding in the caravan mischievously asks Ibn Faḍlān why his God allows such bitter cold. "Because he wants you to say to declare 'There is no god but God'," Ibn Faḍlān tells him in all seriousness. "Well, if we knew Him, we would do it!" comes the playful reply.

Mission to the Volga excels as one man's very personal account of his experiences. It has been mined for valuable nuggets of information about the politics, geography and ethnography of Central Asia in the early fourth/tenth century, and there's a refreshing minimum of hearsay. But the best moments are whenever Ibn Faḍlān puts himself in the picture, telling us what it was like to be confronted by a cheeky and foul-mouthed beggar or to dine in an enormous tent, seated next to a Turkish warlord on a silk covered throne. He is a truly engaging eyewitness. His much-quoted description of the funeral rites of the Rūs on the banks of the Volga has a cinematic quality. It is vivid and unforgettable. You are there with him, watching as the heavily tattooed northmen perform the last rites for one of their chief men. The scene is utterly pagan for a devout Muslim, yet it is to Ibn Faḍlān's credit that he is scrupulous in explaining that the Rūs consider cremation to be better than burial in the earth.

We have no idea what eventually happened to Ibn Faḍlān. Presumably he got home in one piece or we wouldn't have his narrative to enjoy. But it is safe to say that he must have been very glad to be back in familiar, more comfortable surroundings . . . and he has left us with a classic of travel writing.

Tim Severin
West Cork, Ireland

Acknowledgments

I first read sections of Ibn Faḍlān's book as an undergraduate at the University of Glasgow, in the company of John N. Mattock, a guide well seasoned in the classical Arabic tradition. When I began teaching at the University of Oslo in 1992, it seemed only natural that I should guide my students through the description of their Viking forebears. I have read the text in the company of many students at Oslo and Cambridge over the years and learned much from their insights. I would like to thank them all. I can no longer recall what is mine and what is theirs. I guess that's the camaraderie of the road. The same is true of the audiences at the many institutions where I have talked about Ibn Faḍlān and his journey over the years.

When I finished *The Vagaries of the Qaṣīdah* in 1997, I was keen to take a holiday from pre-Islamic poetry, and Ibn Faḍlān's text seemed like just the site I was looking to visit. I did not intend my stay there to become permanent but, in odd ways, it has. Over the years I have written articles and encyclopedia entries, given papers and radio talks, and received many emails and phone calls from those who have also fallen under the spell of the text. I especially remember the Icelander who lost his patience with me when I tried to explain that Crichton's *Eaters of the Dead* was a fantasy novel. Of course, I was hoist with my own petard some years later, when, in the days before library catalogues could be searched electronically, I tried in vain to locate a reference to an article in a journal. I had scribbled it on a piece of paper with no indication as to where I had come across it. After an hour among the catalogues and stacks I realized that the reference was spurious and that it had come from Crichton's preface to the novel!

I have kept up my interest in Ibn Faḍlān as a hobby over the years. I have never found the time to learn Russian, so I knew that I was not the person to do justice to the text and its abundant scholarship. So, I have tried, with my edition and translation, to furnish a new generation of scholars with the basic equipment and the grid references they need to find their way through Ibn Faḍlān's strange but enthralling world.

Many companions have helped me along the way. An old friend, Geert Jan van Gelder, reviewed my first draft a decade ago and, as is his wont, saved me on many occasions from having egg on my chin before I even left the house. A new friend, Shady Hekmat Nasser, advised on orthography. Thorir Jonson Hraundal, of Reykjavik University, helped with the Glossary and the Further Reading. I am delighted that Ibn Faḍlān has afforded us the opportunity to develop our friendship over the years. Maaike van Berkel gave me a copy of her excellent PhD thesis.

Most of the work on this volume has been done on flights between London and Abu Dhabi or New York, in the InterContinental Hotel Abu Dhabi, and in various restaurants, hotels, and bars in Greenwich Village and SoHo. I would like to thank the staff of the InterCon and the cabin crews of Etihad and Virgin Airways who looked after me so well. I can well imagine how envious but dismissive of these luxuries Ibn Faḍlān would be.

Over the years the village of Embsay in Yorkshire has been a welcome retreat where I can combine walking and writing. David and Julie Perrins are wonderful hosts. Nigel Chancellor and Christina Skott took Yvonne and me around the Gulf of Bothnia in their boat and introduced us to the magic of the Finnish sauna. We also managed to explore a Viking cemetery together, despite the depredations of man-eating Finnish insects.

My family has always given me everything I needed, whatever jaunt I was off on.

Philip Kennedy and I have been swapping traveler's tales of our mishaps in the Arabic literary tradition for thirty years. In the company of our editor comrades, we are happily trying to redraw the map of Arabic literary creativity by means of the Library of Arabic Literature. My fellow editors on the board of Library of Arabic Literature are a constant reminder to me of how far I still have to travel in order to master Arabic and English.

And last but by no means least, I owe a special debt to my project editor Shawkat Toorawa. He and I have worked on this volume on and off whenever we happened to be together over eighteen months, and especially in Abu Dhabi in February 2014. There was a delightful incongruity about discussing the frozen wastelands of the Ustyurt beside the pool at the InterCon. And, as with all adventures, my memories of our collaboration will remain with me forever.

Despite such generous guidance and company, I am only too conscious of how often I have stumbled and slipped in my edition, translation and notes. Sometimes I just never learn.

Introduction

On Thursday, the twelfth of Safar, 309 [June 21, 921], a band of intrepid travelers left Baghdad, the City of Peace. Their destination was the confluence of the upper Volga and the Kama, the realm of the king of the Volga Bulghārs. They arrived at the court of the king on Sunday, the twelfth of Muharram, 310 [May 12, 922]. They had been on the road for 325 days and had covered a distance of about 3,000 miles (4,800 km). They must have managed to travel on average about ten miles a day.

The way there was far from easy. The province of Khurasan was in military turmoil. There were many local potentates, such as the Samanid governor of Khwārazm, who were often lukewarm in their support for the caliphate in Baghdad: our travelers had to secure their permission to continue. The Turkish tribes who lived on the Ustyurt plateau, on the eastern shores of the Caspian Sea, were mostly tolerant of Muslim merchants, but they were proudly independent and suspicious of outside interference. The Khazars, who controlled the delta where the Volga flowed into the Caspian, had always defied Muslim control. And there was the terrain and the weather: deserts, mountains, rivers, snows, and bitter cold.

Why would someone want to make such a journey in the early fourth/tenth century, from the luxurious splendor of caliphal Baghdad to a billet in a yurt among the Bulghārs, a semi-nomadic Turkic tribe?

Some months before the travelers left, a missive had reached the court of Caliph al-Muqtadir (r. 295–320/908–32). The king of the

Volga Bulghārs had embraced Islam. He was asking to be accepted as one of the caliph's loyal emirs—the caliph's name would be proclaimed as part of Friday prayers in Bulghār territory. The king petitioned the caliph to send him instruction in law and in how he and his people were to correctly perform religious devotions as proper Muslims. He also asked that the caliph bestow enough funds on him to enable him to construct a fort and thus protect himself against his enemies.

The petition was granted, and arrangements were made to meet the king's request. A diplomatic mission was assembled to visit the king and formally recognize him and his people as members of the Islamic community.

We know about the events and its actors from a remarkable book by Aḥmad ibn Faḍlān, a member of the mission. Yet all of the members of the diplomatic mission remain shrouded in obscurity, especially the book's author.

Sadly our other extant sources make no mention of this adventure. We rely exclusively on the information provided in the book to enable us to reconstruct the composition of the embassy. The only other early source that mentions any of the characters involved is an annalistic chronicle known as *Experiences of Nations, Consequences of Ambition* (*Tajārib al-umam wa-ʿawāqib al-himam*), by the civil servant, philosopher, and historian Miskawayh (d. 421/1030), and, even then, not in the context of the embassy but of the affairs of the reign of al-Muqtadir.

Dramatis Personae

It is difficult to work out from Ibn Faḍlān's book who took part in the mission and who played what part.

1. The Representative: Nadhīr al-Ḥaramī. The man placed in charge of the embassy, who did not actually travel, was the official assigned to recruit the personnel and finance the mission. He seems to have enjoyed al-Muqtadir's confidence,

and it is likely, from his name "al-Ḥaramī," that he was a eunuch who guarded the harem. In addition to organizing the embassy, he entrusted it with (at least) two letters: one was addressed to Atrak ibn al-Qaṭaghān, the field marshal of the Ghuzziyyah (Oghuz Turks), along with several gifts; the other was addressed to the king of the Bulghārs. It is clear from the account that Nadhīr had been in communication with the field marshal and with the Bulghār king. His relationship with the Ghuzziyyah is based on their host-friend system, described in the text, and the Bulghār king had written to him asking for more medication (this is an otherwise unattested detail that features prominently in some non-Arabic accounts of the Bulghārs' conversion to Islam).

2. The Envoy: Sawsan al-Rassī. Sawsan is bound to Nadhīr as his freed man. Sawsan's name "al-Rassī" is obscure but may indicate that he was of Turkic or other Central Asian origin. Sawsan would presumably have been well acquainted with the geopolitics of the region. We discover, when the embassy leaves al-Jurjāniyyah for the Ustyurt, that he is accompanied by a brother-in-law, who is not mentioned elsewhere in the account.
3. The Local Expert: Takīn al-Turkī. Takīn (the name is a Turkic honorific) was well acquainted with and known in the area. The *khwārazm-shāh*, the Samanid governor of Khwārazm, recognizes him and refers to him as a slave-soldier and notes that he had been involved in the arms trade with the Turks, suspecting that he is the prime mover behind the mission. On the Ustyurt, we meet him chatting with a fellow Turk, and, in the enforced stay in Bulghār, he informs Ibn Faḍlān of the presence there of a giant from the land of Gog and Magog.
4. The Soldier: Bārs al-Ṣaqlābī. Bārs may have been the Samanid commander, the chamberlain of Ismāʿīl ibn Aḥmad and governor of al-Jurjāniyyah, who defected, in 296/908–9, with a force of some 4,000 Turkish slave-troops from the Samanids

to Baghdad. Ibn Faḍlān's account provides no substantial information on him.

5. The Financier: A further member of the mission is Aḥmad ibn Mūsā al-Khwārazmī, who is appointed as the agent for the estate from which the mission is to receive its principal funds. Unaccountably, he leaves Baghdad later than the embassy and is easily thwarted in his attempts to reach Bukhara. The mission, therefore, must proceed without the funds the king of the Bulghārs so badly wanted.
6. The vizier Ḥāmid ibn al-ʿAbbās, who otherwise does not feature in our account, has entrusted the mission with a letter for the king.
7. The king is represented by a Khazar: ʿAbdallāh ibn Bāshtū, the Bulghār envoy, was a Muslim of Khazar origin, who may, according to some scholars, have been involved in the dissemination of Islam throughout Volga Bulgharia. The French scholar of Ibn Faḍlān, Marius Canard, thinks he is a political refugee from Khazaria and sees in his ethnic identity a clear indication that Khazar enmity was the occasion of the Bulghār petition.[1] From his actions in Khwārazm, it is clear that ʿAbdallāh's advice was respected by the mission.
8. The jurists and the instructors. These nameless individuals are an enigma. When the mission is about to set out from al-Jurjāniyyah, we discover that there is only one instructor and one jurist. The jurist and the instructor decide not to continue to Bulghār territory. No reason is given.
9. The retainers or slave-soldiers. It also appears, from the report of the departure from al-Jurjāniyyah, that the mission was accompanied by retainers or slave-soldiers (*ghilmān*), who likewise do not continue. This is the sole reference to them in the account.
10. The guide. The mission picks up a guide named Falūs, from al-Jurjāniyyah. It is not clear whether this guide also acts as the *tarjumān*, the interpreter.

11. The interpreter. Ibn Faḍlān mentions "the interpreter" in twelve paragraphs: §§19, 20, 30, 31, 38, 40, 45, 47, 61, 84, 85, 88. It is unclear how many interpreters there are. The king's interpreter was presumably ʿAbdallāh ibn Bāshtū al-Khazarī, whom he sent to Baghdad with his petition, although the text does not say that he fulfilled this function for the king. We also meet Takīn al-Turkī acting in the role of interpreter. Were there more interpreters, one the mission brought along with it as the "guide" from al-Jurjāniyyah and one serving the king of the Bulghārs? The interpreter not only translates on behalf of the embassy but also provides cultural commentary on some of the phenomena and customs observed by Ibn Faḍlān.
12. And so to Ibn Faḍlān, a figure who, like a wandering archetype, turns up in the most unexpected places and in the most unexpected guises. Who was Ibn Faḍlān? As is so often the case, it is easier to begin with who he was not. He was not an Arab merchant, or the leader of the mission, or the secretary of the mission, or a jurist. He was neither the figure inspired by the *Arabian Nights*, whom Michael Crichton created in his novel *The Eaters of the Dead* (1976), nor the Hollywood realization played by Antonio Banderas in the movie *The Thirteenth Warrior* (1999). He was not a Greek resident of Baghdad who had been converted to Islam and held a position of trust at the court of Caliph Muqtadir. In fact, we have only his own words to go by: his role was to ensure that protocol was observed; to read the letters of the caliph, the vizier, and Nadhīr, the representative of the king of the Bulghārs; and to present formally the gifts intended to honor the hosts of the mission. That he was educated is clear from his duties, and the instruction in Islamic law that he delivers to the Muslims of Bulghār would not have been beyond the ken of any reasonably educated Muslim. The king of the Bulghārs treats him as an Arab, though some scholars prefer to see him as a non-Arab Muslim.

At one stage of reading this book, I liked to imagine Ibn Faḍlān as a character not unlike Josiah Harlan, a nineteenth-century American Quaker adventurer in Afghanistan, whose life has now been entertainingly written by Ben Macintyre in *Josiah the Great: The True Story of the Man Who Would Be King.* As Macintyre's title intimates, Harlan is the inspiration for Rudyard Kipling's short story, *The Man Who Would Be King* (first published in *The Phantom Rickshaw*, 1888), wonderfully filmed by John Huston in 1975 with Michael Caine and Sean Connery. Then when I read J.M. Coetzee's remarkable *Waiting for the Barbarians*, I thought I could hear echoes of Ibn Faḍlān in the actions and behavior of Coetzee's Magistrate.

Yet Harlan, Coetzee's Magistrate, and Kipling's Peachey Carnehan and Daniel Drahot are weak adumbrations of Ibn Faḍlān. Ibn Faḍlān is a voice, or, rather, a series of voices: the voice of reason, when faced with his colleagues' obduracy; the voice of decorum and dignity, and often of prudery, when confronted by the wilder excesses of Turkic behavior; the voice of shock, when horrified by the Rūs burial rite. Yet he is also the voice of curiosity, when exposed to the myriad of marvels he witnesses; the voice of candor, when he reveals how he is out-argued by the Bulghār king; and the voice of calm observation, as he tries to remain unperturbed so many miles from home, on the fringes of Muslim eschatology, in the realm of Gog and Magog.

There is something quintessentially human about this series of voices. Like all of us, Ibn Faḍlān can be one person and many simultaneously. He is able to entertain contradictions, as we all are. Our sense of his humanity is highlighted by his avoidance of introspection. He is not given to analysis, whether self-analysis or the analysis of others. He strives to record and understand what he has observed. He regularly fails to understand, as we all do, and sometimes, defeated by what he has observed, he indulges his sense of superiority, as we all do. But he is not convincing when he does so. I find Ibn Faḍlān the most honest of authors writing in the classical

Arabic tradition. His humanity and honesty keep this text fresh and alive for each new generation of readers fortunate to share in its treasures.

My earlier comparison with Kipling is instructive in other ways. Like so much of Kipling's work, for example, the nature of what might loosely be referred to as the imperial experience is at the heart also of Ibn Faḍlān's account—nowhere more acutely, perhaps, than when he is bested in a basic legal disputation (*munāẓarah*) by the Bulghār king or when a Bāshghird tribesman notices our author watching him eating a louse and provocatively declares it a delicacy. And just as Kipling's English mirrors the wit and pace of the table talk enjoyed in the Punjab Club, Ibn Faḍlān's Arabic may perhaps mirror the conversational idioms of his intended audience (or audiences). There is mystery here though. Ibn Faḍlān's audience remains as elusive as do he and the members of the mission, for his work disappears completely without a trace until, several centuries later, the geographer and lexicographer Yāqūt quotes it on his visit to Marw and Khwārazm. In Islamic scholarship, for an author to be read was for that author to be reproduced and quoted. There is no indication that Ibn Faḍlān's work was ever read before Yāqūt!

Turmoil

The world Ibn Faḍlān lived in and traveled through was in turmoil. The caliphal court, the treasury, the vizierate, the provinces, Baghdad's population, religious sectarianism—everything was in a state of upheaval. In Ibn Faḍlān's account we read of the strange surprises and uncustomary peoples he encountered, but he says almost nothing about Baghdad. As Baghdad and the caliphal court provide the religio-political context for the mission, no matter how eastward looking it may be, it is worth visiting Baghdad in the early fourth/tenth century.

Baghdad was the Abbasid capital founded by Caliph al-Manṣūr in 145/762, with its Round City known as the City of Peace (*Madīnat al-Salām*), a Qur'anic echo at its spiritual heart. The Baghdad of the early fourth/tenth century is the Baghdad of al-Muqtadir's reign. At the age of thirteen, al-Muqtadir was the youngest of the Abbasids to become caliph, and he remained caliph for some twenty-four years, with two minor interruptions totaling three days.

A period of stability and possibly even prosperity, one might imagine—but not according to modern scholarship, which views al-Muqtadir's caliphate as an unmitigated disaster, a period when the glorious achievements of his ancestors such as Hārūn al-Rashīd were completely undone.[2] State and caliphal treasuries were bedeviled by chronic lack of funds, with variable revenues from tax and trade. Caliphs and their viziers were constantly caught short of ready money. The fortunes of the recent caliphs had teetered constantly on the brink of bankruptcy.

Upon al-Muqtadir's accession to the caliphate, the rule of al-Muktafī (289–95/902–8) had witnessed a revival in the establishment of caliphal control. The western provinces, Syria and Egypt, had been brought into line, the Qarmaṭians had been defeated by Waṣīf ibn Sawārtakīn the Khazar (294/906–7), and the coffers of the treasury were adequately stocked, to the sum of 15 million dinars.[3]

During al-Muqtadir's caliphate, however, the center once again began to lose its grip on the periphery. Egypt became the private preserve of the rival Faṭimid caliphate, Syria began to enjoy the protection of the Kurdish Ḥamdanid dynasty, and the Qarmaṭian threat erupted once more, in a series of daring raids on cities and caravans, culminating in the theft of the Black Stone from the Kaaba in 317/930, by the Qarmaṭian chieftain Abū Ṭāhir Sulaymān. The eastern provinces had already consolidated the autonomy of their rule. Armenia and Azerbaijan had become the exclusive domains of the caliphally appointed governor Muḥammad ibn Abī l-Sāj al-Afshīn, until his death in 288/901. Transoxania and, by 287/900, Khurasan were under Samanid rule, and Sīstān was the seat of the Ṣaffarids (247–393/861–1003), founded by the coppersmith Ya'qūb ibn al-Layth, a frontier warrior (*mutaṭawwiʿ*) fighting the unbelievers to extend the rule of Islam.

In 309/921, the year the Volga mission left Baghdad, al-Muqtadir's reign did enjoy some military success, when Mu'nis, the supreme commander of the caliphal armies, was invested with the governorship of Egypt and Syria, and the Samanids gained an important victory over the Daylamites of Ṭabaristān and killed al-Ḥasan ibn al-Qāsim's governor of Jurjān, the redoubtable Daylamite warlord Līlī ibn al-Nuʿmān, near Ṭūs, an event to which Ibn Faḍlān refers (§4).

The treasury's fiscal and mercantile revenues were heavily dependent on the success of the caliphal army, and no stability could be guaranteed. Apparently al-Muqtadir did not care in the least about stability: he is reputed to have squandered more than seventy million dinars.[4]

The dazzling might and splendor of the imperial Baghdad of al-Muqtadir's reign were fabulously encapsulated in his palace complexes. I like in particular the spectacular Arboreal Mansion. This mansion housed a tree of eighteen branches of silver and gold standing in a pond of limpid water. Birds of gold and silver, small and large, perched on the twigs. The branches would move, and their leaves would move as if stirred by the wind. The birds would tweet, whistle, and coo. On either side of the mansion were arranged fifteen automata, knights on horseback, who performed a cavalry maneuver. The lavishness of this craftsmanship and the ingenuity of its engineering match the opulence of the caliphal architectural expenditure for which al-Muqtadir was rightly famed. The Arboreal Mansion was just one of the many awe-inspiring sights of the caliphal complex (which included a zoo, a lion house, and an elephant enclosure) on the left bank of the Tigris: one observer reckoned it to be the size of the town of Shiraz.

Al-Muqtadir remained caliph for many years, and his longevity was accompanied by a decline in administrative consistency. Fourteen different administrators held the office of vizier during the period. This was one of the secrets behind the length of al-Muqtadir's rule: he, with the complicity of his bureaucracy, was following the precedent set by Hārūn al-Rashīd when, in 187/803,

Hārūn so spectacularly and inexplicably removed the Barmakid family from power. The financial expedient of *muṣādarah* ("mulcting": the confiscation of private ministerial fortunes, a procedure usually accompanied by torture and beating) contributed to these changes, with courtly conspiracy and collusion the order of the day. We have an example of this in Ibn Faḍlān's account, for the funds to cover the construction of the fort in Bulghār territory were to be acquired from the sale of an estate owned by a deposed vizier, Ibn al-Furāt (§§3, 5).

Baghdad, with its population of between a quarter and half a million people in the fourth/tenth century, was the world's largest consumer of luxury goods, and trade was buoyant, but it was also a city on the brink of lawlessness and anarchy. It was poorly managed, food supplies were unreliable, famine was a regular occurrence, and prices were high. There were sporadic outbreaks of disease, largely because of the floods occasioned by municipal neglect of the irrigation system.

Factionalism was commonplace, and religious animosities, especially those between the Shiʿi community and the Ḥanbalite Sunnis, under the energetic direction of the theologian and traditionist al-Ḥasan ibn ʿAlī ibn Khalaf al-Barbahārī (d. 329/941), frequently erupted into violence. Although doctrinally quietist and sternly opposed to formal political rebellion, the Ḥanbalites, followers of Aḥmad ibn Ḥanbal (d. 241/855), did not disregard divergent expressions of Islamic belief or public displays of moral laxity. They took to the streets of Baghdad on several occasions to voice their disapproval of the corruption of the times. The great jurist, exegete, and historian al-Ṭabarī (d. 310/923) is thought to have incurred their wrath when he pronounced a compromise verdict on a theological dispute concerning the precise implications of Q Isrāʾ 17:79:

> Strive through the night—as an offering in hope that your
> Lord may raise you to a praiseworthy place.

This verse had been adopted by al-Barbahārī as a slogan, following the realist and anthropomorphic exegesis of it advocated by his teacher, al-Marwazī (d. 275/888). According to the Ḥanbalites, the verse declared that God would physically place Muḥammad on His throne on Judgment Day—anything less was tantamount to heresy. According to several sources, Ḥanbalite animosity to al-Ṭabarī persisted until his death, when a mob gathered at his home and prevented a public funeral being held in his honor. Al-Ṭabarī was buried in his home, under cover of darkness.

Ḥanbalite agitation was at its most violent in 323/935, when the caliph al-Rāḍī (r. 322–29/934–40) was compelled formally to declare Ḥanbalism a heresy and to exclude the Ḥanbalites from the Islamic community.

And then the authorities had al-Ḥallāj to contend with. Abū l-Mughīth al-Ḥusayn ibn Manṣūr, known as al-Ḥallāj, "the Wool-Carder," was a charismatic Sufi visionary. In the markets of Baghdad he preached a message of God as the One Truth, the Only Desire. He installed a replica of the Kaaba in his house and passed the night in prayer in graveyards. He appealed to the populace to kill him and save him from God, and, in a fateful encounter in the Mosque of al-Manṣūr in Baghdad, he is said to have exclaimed, "I am the Truth." In other words, he shouted, he had no other identity than God.

The administration was terrified of the revolutionary appeal of al-Ḥallāj and considered him a threat to the stability of the empire. He was arrested and an inquisition held. His main opponents were Ibn al-Furāt and Ḥāmid ibn al-ʿAbbās, both of whom feature in Ibn Faḍlān's account. (It was one of Ibn al-Furāt's estates that was to fund the building of the Bulghār fort, and Ḥāmid ibn al-ʿAbbās provided the mission with a letter for the king of the Bulghārs.) It was a singular event to see both men in agreement in their opposition to al-Ḥallāj. They so hated one another that, when Ibn al-Furāt had been accused of financial corruption and removed from the vizierate, Ḥāmid, who was to replace him, was restrained from a vicious attempt to pull out Ibn al-Furāt's beard! Al-Ḥallāj was executed on March 26, 922, two months before the mission reached the Bulghārs.[5]

It was from this "City of Peace" that the embassy departed, following the Khurasan highway, but the first leg of their journey was fraught with danger. They made their way to Rayy, the commercial capital of al-Jibāl province. In military terms, this was one of the most hotly contested cities in the whole region. In 311/919, two years before the departure of the mission, Ibn Faḍlān's patron Muḥammad ibn Sulaymān had been killed in a failed attempt to oust the Daylamite Aḥmad ibn ʿAlī from control of the city. Aḥmad ibn ʿAlī was later formally invested by Baghdad as governor of Rayy (307–11/919–24). At the time of the mission, then, the caliphate, the Samanids, and the Zaydī Daylamites were engaged in constant struggle for control of the region.

There were other powerful local actors at work in the area, too. Ibn Abī l-Sāj, the governor of Azerbaijan, was a force to be reckoned with. So too was Ibn Qārin, the ruler of Firrīm and the representative of the Caspian Zaydī *dāʿī* al-Ḥasan ibn al-Qāsim. Al-Ḥasan ibn al-Qāsim was the successor to al-Uṭrūsh ("the Deaf") (d. 304/917), restorer of Zaydī Shiʿism in Ṭabaristān and Daylam. Both were powerful men hostile to Abbasids and Samanids. This is why Ibn Faḍlān notes, with some relief, that Līlī ibn Nuʿmān, a Daylamite warlord in the service of al-Uṭrūsh and al-Ḥasan ibn al-Qāsim, had been killed shortly before the embassy reached Nishapur (§4), and why he points out that, in Nishapur, they encountered a friendly face in Ḥammawayh Kūsā, Samanid field marshal of Khurasan. The mission thus made its way briskly through a dangerous region and, in order to proceed to Bukhara, successfully negotiated its first major natural obstacle, the Karakum desert.

Such was the world in which the caliphal envoys lived and against which Ibn Faḍlān would measure the peoples and persons he met on his way to the Volga.

Why?

Why did Caliph al-Muqtadir agree to the king's petition? What did the court seek to achieve? What were the motives behind the mission? The *khwārazm-shāh* in Kāth (Khwārazm) (§8) and the four chieftains of the Ghuzziyyah assembled by Atrak ibn al-Qaṭaghān (§33) are suspicious of Baghdad's interest in spreading Islam among the Bulghār. The Samanid emir shows no interest in the mission. He was still a teenager, after all (§5). Should we be suspicious too or emulate the teenage emir?

The king asked the caliph for instruction in Islamic law and ritual practice, a mosque and a *minbar* to declare his fealty to the caliph as part of the Friday prayer, and the construction of a fort. The Baghdad court's reasons for acceding to the request are not specified. There is no discussion in the account of the lucrative trade route that linked Baghdad, Bukhara, and Volga Bulgharia; of the emergence of the Bulghār market as a prime source of furs and slaves; or of the Viking lust for silver dirhams that largely fuelled the northern fur and slave trade. Yet there are hints. We learn of the political and religious unrest in Khurasan (bad for the secure passage of trade goods), of the autonomy of the Samanid emirate in Bukhara, and of how jealously the trade links between Bukhara, Khwārazm, and the Turks of the north were protected by the Samanid governor of Khwārazm.

Scholars have speculated on the motives of the mission. Was it intended somehow to bypass the Samanid emirate and secure the Bulghār market for Baghdad? International diplomacy did not exist in isolation but was in many ways the official handmaiden of mercantile relations. Trade was fundamental to the economies of the northern frontier and also a factor in the commission of the embassy: a fort, along the lines of Sarkel on the Don, would have provided the Muslims with a stronghold from which to resist the Khazars and control the flow of trade through the confluence of the Volga and the Kama and would have been a statement of Islamic presence in the area. Or is this speculation just the imposition on the fourth/tenth century of our own obsessions with economic viability?

For Shaban, this diplomatic adventure was a "full-fledged trade mission . . . a response to a combined approach by Jayhānī and the chief of the Bulghār." Shaban thinks the Volga mission was a cooperative venture between the Samanids and Abbasids masterminded by al-Jayhānī, an assertion for which there is no shred of evidence. He reasons that the Samanids needed allies to help control the Turkic tribes north of Khwārazm.[6]

Togan, who discovered the Mashhad manuscript in 1923, suggested that conversion to Islam as conceived and practiced by the caliphal court in such a distant outpost of the empire would have acted as a corrective to Qarmaṭian propaganda, to Zoroastrian prophecies of the collapse of the caliphate at the hands of the Majūs (a name, in Arabic texts of the period, for fire-worshippers, i.e., both Zoroastrians and Vikings!), and to Shiʿi missionary activity, and would have countered the spread of any of these influences among the already volatile Turkic tribes.[7] Togan was a Bashkir Bolshevik who had fallen out with Lenin over policies concerning Togan's native Tataristan and was living in exile in Iran. It is hardly surprising that he read the mission in such richly ideological terms.

According to one commentator, the court must have reasoned that, by controlling how the Volga Bulghārs observed Islamic ritual, it could control their polity, a position that owes more to modern notions of political Islam than to an understanding of the fourth/tenth century.[8]

Do we need to be so suspicious? Of course, the religious overtones of the king's petitions were sure to appeal to the caliph and his court. Here was a foreign ruler who had embraced Islam, requesting religious instruction, as well as the construction of a mosque and a *minbar* from which he could acknowledge the caliph's suzerainty, and seeking assistance against unspecified enemies, presumably the Khazars, although the Rus' always represented a threat. The construction of a fort on the Volga bend would have followed the precedents set by both Rørik's hill-fort, built by the Rus', and Sarkel, built on the Don by the Byzantines for the Khazars.

It might be helpful to take a brief look at some disparate examples of the Christian ideology of trade, travel, warfare, and expansion. In 1433, Dom Manuel justifies the Portuguese voyages of discovery:

> not only with the intention that great fame and profit might follow to these kingdomes from the riches that there are therein, which were always possessed by the Moors, but so that the faith of Our Lord should be spread through more parts, and His Name known.[9]

Jonathan Riley-Smith has argued that religion and self-interest were inseparable in the outlook of the early Crusaders.[10] Stephen Greenblatt discusses the "formalism" of Columbus's "linguistic acts," and Margarita Zamora draws attention to the equal weight given spiritual and worldly (i.e., commercial) ambitions in the "Letter to the Sovereigns."[11] Christopher Hill has been the most persistent and persuasive exponent of the religiosity of the seventeenth-century Puritan worldview, in which every aspect of man's behavior is seen through a religious prism.[12] In the wake of the feting of William Dampier upon the publication of his *New Voyage round the World* in 1697, the Royal Society urged seamen to greater scientific precision in their journals, "to improve the stock of knowledge in the world and hence improve the condition of mankind."[13] And by improving "the condition of mankind," we can savor the ambiguity between Enlightenment reason and the *mission civilatrice* that would come with conversion to Christianity.

It is muddle-headed to consider religious motives as mere justification for interference in "foreign" affairs. The caliphal court would not have known what we mean by these distinctions. Such a line of reasoning attempts to separate and differentiate between a mutually inclusive set of notions: missionary activity, conversion, trade, and expansion of the caliphate. What I am advocating is respect for the integrity of Ibn Faḍlān's account.

Yāqūt's Quotations

The Arabic text of Ibn Faḍlān's book exists in two formats: as part of a manuscript contained in the library attached to the Mausoleum of the imam ʿAlī al-Riḍā in Mashhad, Iran, discovered in 1923 by A. Zeki Validi Togan (the text translated in this book as *Mission to the Volga*); and as six quotations in Yāqūt's *Muʿjam al-buldān* (*Dictionary of Places*) (also translated in this book).

Yāqūt ibn ʿAbdallāh al-Rūmī al-Ḥamawī (574-75–626/1179–1229) was a biographer and geographer renowned for his encyclopedic writings. "Al-Rūmī" ("the man from Rūm") refers to his Byzantine descent, and "al-Ḥamawī" connects him with Ḥāmah, in Syria. In his topographical dictionary *Kitab Muʿjam al-buldān*, he included quotations from Ibn Faḍlān's account, which remained the principal vestiges of the work until Togan's discovery of the Mashhad manuscript in 1923.

The geographical dictionary of Yāqūt includes excerpts from Ibn Faḍlān's book in six lemmata:

1. Itil: Wüstenfeld 1.112.16–113.15 = Mashhad 208a.4–208b.9 → §68 of the present translation.
2. Bāshghird: Wüstenfeld 1.468.17–469.15 = Mashhad 203a.7–203b.3 → §§37–38 of the present translation.
3. Bulghār: Wüstenfeld 1.723.6–19 = Mashhad 196b.18–197a.12; 1.723.19–724.9 = Mashhad 203b.5–204a.3; 1.724.9–725.4 = 204a.4–204b.7; 1.725.5–726.16 = 205b.1–206a.12; 1.726.16–727.1 = 206b.2–10; 1.727.2–3 = 206b.14–16; 1.727.3–10 = 206b.17–207a.5; 1.727.10–12 = 207a.9–11; 1.727.12–13 = 207a.16–17; 1.727.14–21 = 207b.4–11; → §§2–4, 39–44, 48–50, 51, 53–56, 59, 61–63 respectively of the present translation.
4. Khazar: Wüstenfeld 2.436.20–440.6 (only 2.438.11–14 matches the extant text in the Mashhad manuscript) = Mashhad 212b.15–19 = §90 of the present translation.

5. Khwārazm: Wüstenfeld 2.484.10–485.23 = Mashhad 198a.17–199a.3 = §§8–11 of the present translation.
6. Rūs: Wüstenfeld 2.834.18–840.12 = Mashhad 209b.17–212b.15 =. §§74–89 of the present translation.

Yāqūt frequently remarks that he has abbreviated Ibn Faḍlān's account, occasionally criticizes him, and expresses disbelief in his version of events. He stresses that his quotation of Ibn Faḍlān's passage on the Rūs is accurate and implies that it is a verbatim quotation. This raises, in my mind, the possibility that Yāqūt may not be quoting Ibn Faḍlān so accurately in the other five lemmata. And a close comparison between the passages on the Rūs in both sources reveals that, here too, Yāqūt's quotation may not, strictly speaking, be verbatim but may have been subjected to modification, paraphrasing, and rewording. (I say "may have been" because it is likely that Yāqūt was quoting from an ancestor to the actual Mashhad manuscript.) Furthermore, in the lemma devoted to the Khazars, Yāqūt confuses quotations drawn from al-Iṣṭakhrī's mid-fourth/tenth century work *Kitāb al-Masālik wa-l-mamālik* (*The Book of Highways and Kingdoms*) with the quotation he took from Ibn Faḍlān, although it is also possible that this section of the Khazars has been taken from al-Iṣṭakhrī's text and added to Ibn Faḍlān's account by the compiler of the Mashhad manuscript.

For the sake of completeness and in order to make clear the differences between Yāqūt's versions and the work translated as *Mission to the Volga*, I include Yāqūt's quotations from Ibn Faḍlān translated from Wüstenfeld's edition; please note, I have not consulted any of the manuscripts of Yāqūt's *Muʿjam al-buldān* but have relied instead on Wüstenfeld's edition. In order to facilitate comparison between these quotations and the version of the text contained in the Mashhad manuscript, I have included in the translation of these quotations the paragraph numbers from *Mission to the Volga* to which Yāqūt's quotations correspond.[14]

Ibn Faḍlān's Logbook: An Imagined Reconstruction

I present here a shortened version of Ibn Faḍlān's text, an experiment in reconstructing the logbook that I imagine Ibn Faḍlān might have kept while on his travels. My version of the logbook ends abruptly. Of course this is an imagined reconstruction and I could have terminated it at the beginning of the list of Bulghār marvels (to which the description of the Rūs belongs).[15]

Names

One of the wonderful things about Ibn Faḍlan's account is that we get to hear about so many unfamiliar places and, in the process, are introduced to many Turkic terms transcribed (presumably aurally and phonetically) into Arabic, and to listen to so many non-Arabs speak, via the intermediary of the translator(s) Ibn Faḍlān used. Of course, this abundance of transcriptions is rarely graphically straightforward.

There is confusion surrounding the "correct" form of the toponyms and Turkic titles in which the text abounds. Whenever possible I have relied on the many studies of Turkic names and titles by scholars such as Peter Golden. The onomastic challenge is especially acute in the riverine topography of the journey from the Ghuzziyyah to the Bulghārs: §§34–38. A uniform solution to these names proved impossible, so I decided to apply a principle of minimal intervention. When the identity of the river proposed by scholars seemed close to the form of the word as written by the Mashhad scribe I accepted the reconstructed identification and made as few changes as possible to the form of the name given in the manuscript. The principle of minimal intervention means, for example, that the word *swḥ* becomes *sūḥ* and not *sūkh*, and *bājā'* does not become *bājāgh*. Please note, however, that *ḥ*j* (the "*" is used here and in a few other cases to represent an undotted consonant in the manuscript that could be read as *bā'*, *tā'*, *thā'*, *nūn*, or *yā'*) became *jaykh*. I have avoided, wherever possible, the addition of vowels to the consonantal skeleton of these names. On one occasion I could not decide whether the word *smwr* masked *s-mūr* or *s-mawr*, so I let it stand.

This procedure of minimal intervention is not an argument for the onomastic accuracy of the manuscript. There has undoubtedly been considerable corruption in transmission, and the scribe of the Mashhad manuscript is not always as reliable as we might like. The procedure is simply a not very subtle solution to an impasse. I use the Glossary of Names and Terms to discuss Turkic terms and names and to survey the identifications offered by scholars.

In the two cases in which we are fortunate to have lemmata in Yāqūt's *Muʿjam al-buldān* (Itil and Arthakhushmīthan), I have adopted his orthography and vocalization.

My Translation

Ibn Faḍlan's text is brisk and characterized by narrative economy. I wanted my English to be the same. My translation aspires to lucidity and legibility. James E. McKeithen's excellent PhD thesis (Indiana University, 1979) will satisfy the reader in search of a crib of the Arabic. There are two other translations into English, by Richard N. Frye (2005) and by the late Paul Lunde and Caroline Stone (2012). They are both admirable: Frye's is very useful for the studies he provides alongside the translation, and Lunde and Stone have produced a nicely readable version of the work. Both, however, effectively promote a version of Ibn Faḍlān's text dominated by Yāqūt's quotations.

I have also added to the translation some headers, toponyms, and ethnonyms that help identify the principal agents and locations of the action.

The Guide to Further Reading is intended to provide readers, students, and scholars interested in studying the work further with a representative catalogue of secondary scholarship on Ibn Faḍlān and his world. For ease of reference, it is therefore organized according to subject. I hope this will be a useful study aid to what can sometimes be a complicated bibliographical tumult.

I have also prepared the Glossary as a repository of information that, in a publication intended for an academic audience, might be included in the form of annotations to the text. This approach has the added advantage of keeping to a minimum both the glossary and the annotation to the translation. Each glossary entry includes key references to the copious annotations provided by the scholars who have edited and/or translated the work. I hope that, in this way too, this version of the glossary can become a useful study aid.

Conclusion

To be sure, Ibn Faḍlan's account is in many ways a strange book. It has no textual analogues, no other works from the third/ninth or fourth/tenth centuries we can compare it with. Its obsession with eyewitness testimony, connected ultimately with the practice of, and requirements for, giving witness in a court of law, is almost pathological. It contains many wonderful encounters, conversations, dialogues, and formal audiences—and we hear so many non-Muslims speak, from tribesmen of the Ghuzziyyah and the Bulghār king to the Rūs who mocks Ibn Faḍlān for the primitiveness of his religious observances. On top of all this, it is a cracking good read. I hope others enjoy reading it as much as I have enjoyed translating it and, along the way, kept alive my boyhood love of adventure stories.

Notes to the Introduction

1 *Relation*, 51.

2 Zettersteén and Bosworth, "al-Muḳtadir," 542; Kennedy, *The Prophet and the Age of the Caliphates*, 188.

3 See Kennedy, *Prophet*, 187; Zettersteén and Bosworth, "al-Muktafī."

4 Zettersteén and Bosworth, "al-Muḳtadir."

5 Massignon and Gardet, "al-Ḥallād̲j̲," 102; Massignon, *Hallāj. Mystic and Martyr*.

6 Shaban, *Islamic History: A New Interpretation*, 2:149–51.

7 *Reisebericht*, xx–xxvii.

8 Bukharaev, *Islam in Russia*, 39.

9 Subrahmanyam, *The Career and Legend of Vasco da Gama*, 170.

10 Riley-Smith, "The State of Mind of Crusaders to the East, 1095–1300."

11 Greenblatt, *Marvelous Possessions*, 53–85; Zamora, "Christopher Columbus's 'Letter to the Sovereigns.'"

12 Hill, *The English Bible and the Seventeenth Century Revolution*, 34.

13 Edwards, *The Story of the Voyage*, 26–27.

14 These quotations are also available, with the corresponding Arabic, on the Library of Arabic Literature Web site.

15 This reconstruction is also available, with the corresponding Arabic, on the Library of Arabic Literature Web site.

Mission to the Volga

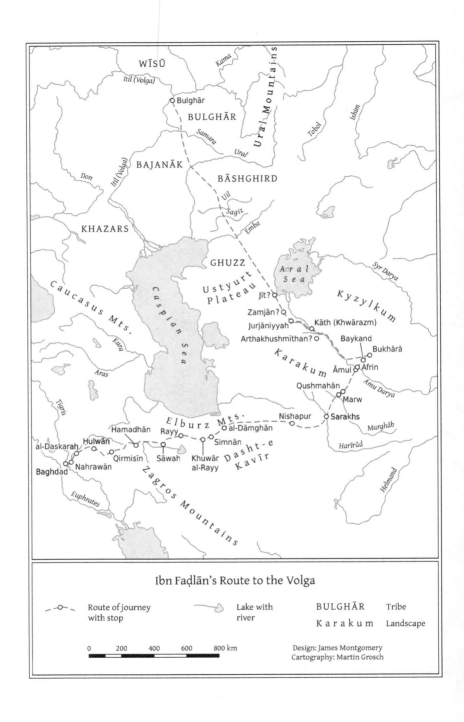

Ibn Faḍlān's Route to the Volga

Route of journey with stop

Lake with river

BULGHĀR Tribe

K a r a k u m Landscape

0 200 400 600 800 km

Design: James Montgomery
Cartography: Martin Grosch

Mission to the Volga

This is the written account of Aḥmad ibn Faḍlān ibn al-ʿAbbās ibn Rāshid[1] ibn Ḥammād, the envoy of al-Muqtadir to the king of the Ṣaqālibah. His patron was Muḥammad ibn Sulaymān.[2] It records his observations in the realm of the Turks, the Khazars, the Rūs, the Ṣaqālibah, the Bāshghird, and other peoples. It also includes reports of their various customs and ways of living, their kings, and many other related matters, too. 1

Aḥmad ibn Faḍlān said:[3] In the letter of al-Ḥasan, son of Yilṭawār, the king of the Ṣaqālibah, which al-Muqtadir the Commander of the Faithful received, the king petitioned al-Muqtadir to send people to instruct him in law and acquaint him with the rules of Islam according to the sharia, and to construct a mosque and build a *minbar* from which he could proclaim al-Muqtadir's name throughout his kingdom. He also beseeched him to build a fort to protect him against the kings who opposed him. His requests were granted. 2

Baghdad

The representative of the king of the Ṣaqālibah at court was Nadhīr al-Ḥaramī.[4] I, Aḥmad ibn Faḍlān, was delegated to read al-Muqtadir's letter to him, to present him with the official gifts designated, and to supervise the jurists and instructors. Nadhīr identified a fixed sum of money to be brought to him, to cover the construction costs and to pay the jurists and instructors. These expenses were to be covered by Arthakhushmīthan, one of the estates of Ibn 3 al-Furāt in Khwārazm. The envoy from the king of the Ṣaqālibah to the caliph was a man named ʿAbdallāh ibn Bāshtū al-Khazarī. The caliph's envoy was Sawsan al-Rassī. Sawsan's patron was Nadhīr al-Ḥaramī. Takīn al-Turkī, Bārs al-Ṣaqlābī, and I accompanied him. As I said, I was charged with the following responsibilities: I presented him with the official gifts for him, his wife, children, brothers, and commanders. I also handed over the medication that the king had requested, in writing, from Nadhīr.[5]

4 We traveled from Baghdad, City of Peace, on Thursday, the twelfth of Safar, 309 [June 21, 921]. We stayed one day in Nahrawān, then rode hard until we reached al-Daskarah, where we stayed three days. Then we traveled without delay or diversion and came to Ḥulwān, where we stayed two days. From there we traveled to Qirmīsīn, where we stayed another two days, and next arrived at Hamadhān, where we stayed three days. We traveled to Sāwah and, after two days, on to Rayy, where we stayed eleven days, until Aḥmad ibn ʿAlī, the brother of Ṣuʿlūk, had left Khuwār al-Rayy. Then we traveled to Khuwār al-Rayy itself and three days later to Simnān, then on to al-Dāmghān, where our caravan happened to encounter Ibn Qārin, who was preaching on behalf of the *dāʿī*. We concealed our identity and hurried to Nishapur, where we met Ḥammawayh Kūsā, the field marshal of Khurasan. Līlī ibn Nuʿmān had just been killed. Then we proceeded to Sarakhs, Marw, and Qushmahān, at the edge of the Āmul desert. We stayed three days there and changed camels for the desert journey. We crossed the desert to Āmul and then reached Āfr*n, the outpost of Ṭāhir ibn ʿAlī, on the other side of the Jayḥūn.[6]

5 *Bukhara*

We traveled via Baykand to Bukhara, where we went straight to al-Jayhānī, the chancellor of the emir of Khurasan, known there as the chief *shaykh*. He had ordered a residence for us and had appointed someone to attend to all our needs and concerns and make sure that we experienced no difficulty in getting what we wanted. After a few days, he arranged an audience with Naṣr ibn

Aḥmad. We discovered that he was still a boy and did not even have a beard. We greeted him as befits an emir. He commanded us to be seated. His very first words were: "How was my patron, the Commander of the Faithful, when you left him? May God give him long life and cherish him, his retinue, and his spiritual companions." "He was well," we replied. He said, "May God increase his well-being!" The letter was then read out to him. It gave the following instructions: the estate of Arthakhushmīthan was to be handed over by al-Faḍl ibn Mūsā al-Naṣrānī, Ibn al-Furāt's agent, to Aḥmad ibn Mūsā al-Khwārazmī; we were to be provided with funds, with a letter to his governor in Khwārazm ordering him not to hinder us, and with a letter to the garrison at the Gate of the Turks, who were to provide us with an escort and not detain us. "Where is Aḥmad ibn Mūsā?" he asked. "We left the City of Peace without him, and he set off four days later,"[7] we replied and he said, "I hear and obey the commands of my patron, the Commander of the Faithful, may God give him long life!"

Ibn Faḍlān said: al-Faḍl ibn Mūsā al-Naṣrānī, Ibn al-Furāt's 6
agent, got wind of this and came up with a plan to deal with Aḥmad ibn Mūsā. He wrote to the deputies of the superintendent of the Khurasan highway, in the military district of Sarakhs-Baykand, as follows: "Tell your spies to keep a lookout for Aḥmad ibn Mūsā in the caravanserais and the lookout posts. Enclosed is his description. The man who catches him is to detain him until we specify the punishment in writing." Aḥmad ibn Mūsā was later arrested in Marw and put in chains. We stayed twenty-eight days in Bukhara. ʿAbdallāh ibn Bāshtū and other members of our party kept saying, "If we tarry, the winter onslaught will mean we will miss the crossing. Aḥmad ibn Mūsā will catch up with us and will join us." Al-Faḍl ibn Mūsā encouraged this.

Ibn Faḍlān said: I noticed in Bukhara that the dirhams were 7
made of different colored metals. One of them, the *ghiṭrīfī* dirham, is made of red and yellow brass. It is accepted according to numerical value rather than weight: one hundred *ghiṭrīfī* dirhams equals

one silver dirham. In the dowries for their womenfolk they make the following stipulations: so-and-so, the son of so-and-so, marries so-and-so, the daughter of so-and-so, for so many thousand *ghiṭrīfī* dirhams. This also applies to the purchase of property and the purchase of slaves—they specifically mention *ghiṭrīfī* dirhams. They have other dirhams, made only of yellow brass, forty of which equal one *dānaq*, and a further type of yellow-brass dirham called the *samarqandī*, six of which equal one *dānaq*.

8 *Khwārazm* I listened to the warnings of ʿAbdallāh ibn Bāshtū and the others about the onslaught of winter. We left Bukhara and returned to the river, where we hired a boat for Khwārazm, more than two hundred *farsakh*s from where we hired the boat. We were able to travel only part of the day. A whole day's travel was impossible because of the cold. When we got to Khwārazm, we were given an audience with the emir, Muḥammad ibn ʿIrāq Khwārazm-Shāh, who gave us a warm and hospitable reception and a place to stay. Three days later, he summoned us, quizzing us about wanting to enter the realm of the Turks. "I cannot let you do that," he said. "I am not permitted to let you risk your lives. I think all this is a ploy devised by this soldier." (He meant Takīn.)[8] "He used to live here as a blacksmith, when he ran the iron trade in the land of the infidels. He is the one who beguiled Nadhīr and got him to speak to the Commander of the Faithful and to bring the letter of the king of the Ṣaqālibah to him. The exalted emir," (he meant the emir of Khurasan) "has more right to have the name of the Commander of the Faithful proclaimed out there, if only he could find a safe way to do it.[9] And then there are a thousand infidel tribes in your path. This is clearly an imposture foisted upon the caliph. Such is my counsel. I now have no recourse but to write to the exalted emir, so that he can write to the caliph (God give him strength!) and consult with him. You will remain here until the answer comes." We left things at that but came back later and pressured him. "We have the orders and the letter of the Commander of the Faithful, so why do you need

to consult?" we said. In the end, he granted us permission and we sailed downriver from Khwārazm to al-Jurjāniyyah. The distance by water is fifty *farsakh*s.

I noticed that the dirhams in Khwārazm are adulterated and should not be accepted, because they are made of lead and brass. They call their dirham a *ṭāzijah*. It weighs four and a half *dānaq*s. The money changers trade in sheep bones, spinning tops, and dirhams. They are the strangest of people in the way they talk and behave. When they talk they sound just like starlings calling. There is a village one day away called Ardkwā, whose inhabitants are called al-Kardaliyyah. When they talk they sound just like frogs croaking. At the end of the prayer they disavow the Commander of the Faithful, ʿAlī ibn Abī Ṭālib, God be pleased with him. 9

Al-Jurjāniyyah

We stayed several days in al-Jurjāniyyah. The River Jayḥūn froze over completely, from beginning to end. The ice was seventeen spans thick. Horses, mules, donkeys, and carts used it like a road and it did not move—it did not even creak. It stayed like this for three months. We thought the country we were visiting was an «infernally cold»[10] portal to the depths of Hell. When snow fell, it was accompanied by a wild, howling blizzard. 10

When people here want to honor each other and be generous they say, "Come to my house so we can talk, for I have a good fire burning." This is their custom for expressing genuine generosity and affability. God the exalted has been kind to them by making firewood plentiful and very cheap: a cart load of *ṭāgh* wood costs only two local dirhams, and their carts can hold about three thousand *raṭl*s. Normally, their beggars do not stand outside at the door but go into the house, sit for a while, and get warm by the fire. Then they say, "Bakand" meaning "bread." 11

We were in al-Jurjāniyyah for a long time: several days of Rajab and all of Shaʿban, Ramadan, and Shawwal.[11] We stayed there so long because the cold was so severe. Indeed, I was told that two men had driven twelve camels to transport a load of firewood from 12 a particular forest but had forgotten to take their flint and tinderbox and passed the night without a fire. In the morning it was so cold that they had frozen to death, as had their camels. The weather was so cold that you could wander round the markets and through the streets and not meet anyone. I would leave the baths, and, by the time I got home, I would look at my beard and see a block of ice. I would have to thaw it at the fire. I would sleep inside a chamber, inside another chamber,[12] with a Turkish yurt of animal skins inside it, and would be smothered in cloaks and pelts, and even then my cheek would sometimes freeze and stick to the pillow. I noticed containers wrapped in sheepskins, to stop them shattering and breaking, but this did them no good at all. I even saw the ground open up into great rifts and mighty, ancient trees split in two because of the cold.

13 Halfway into Shawwal of 309 [February, 922], the season began to change and the Jayḥūn melted. We set about acquiring the items we needed for our journey. We purchased Turkish camels, constructed the camel-skin rafts for crossing all the rivers we had to cross in the realm of the Turks, and packed provisions of bread, millet, and cured meat to last three months. The locals who knew us told us in no uncertain terms to wear proper clothing outdoors and to wear a lot of it. They gave us a terrifying description of the cold and impressed upon us the need to take the matter very, very seriously. But when we experienced it ourselves, it was so much worse than what they had described, even though we each wore a tunic, a caftan, a sheepskin, a horse blanket, and a burnoose with only our eyes showing, a pair of trousers, another pair of lined trousers, leggings, and a pair of animal skin boots with yet another pair on top of them. Mounted on our camels, we wore so many heavy clothes we couldn't move. The jurist, the instructor, and the retainers who had left the City of Peace with us stayed behind, too scared to enter the realm of the Turks. I pushed on with the envoy, his brother-in-law, and the two soldiers, Takīn and Bārs.[13]

On the day we planned to set off, I said to them, "The king's man accompanies you. He knows everything. And you carry the letters of the caliph. They must surely mention the four thousand *musayyabī* dinars intended for the king. You will be at the court of a non-Arab king, and he will demand that you pay this sum." "Don't worry about it," they replied, "he will not ask us for them." "He will demand that you produce them. I know it," I warned. But they paid no heed. The caravan was ready to depart, so we hired a guide called Falūs, an inhabitant of al-Jurjāniyyah. We trusted in almighty God, putting our fate in His hands. 14

We left al-Jurjāniyyah on Monday, the second of Dhu l-Qaʿdah, 309 [Monday, March 4, 922], and stopped at an outpost called Zamjān, the Gate of the Turks. The following morning we traveled as far as a stopping post called Jīt. The snow had fallen so heavily that it came up to the camels' knees. We had to stay there two days. Then we kept a straight course and plunged deep into the realm of the Turks through a barren, mountainless desert. We met no one. We crossed for ten days. Our bodies suffered terrible injuries. We were exhausted. The cold was biting, the snowstorms never-ending. It made the cold of Khwārazm seem like summertime. We forgot all about our previous sufferings and were ready to give up the ghost. 15

One day, the cold was unusually biting. Takīn was traveling beside me, talking in Turkic to a Turk at his side. He laughed and said, "This Turk wants to know, 'What does our Lord want from us? He is killing us with this cold. If we knew what He wanted, then we could just give it to Him.'" "Tell him," I replied, "that He wants you to declare 'There is no god but God.'" "Well, if we knew Him, we'd do it," he said with a laugh.[14] 16

We came to a place where there was a huge quantity of *ṭāgh* wood and stopped. The members of the caravan lit fires and got them going. They took their clothes off and dried them by the fires.[15] Then we departed, traveling as quickly and with as much energy as we could manage, from midnight until the midday or afternoon prayer, when we would stop for a rest. After fifteen nights of this,[16] we came 17 to a huge rocky mountain. Springs of water ran down it and gathered to form a lake at its foot.

18 *The Ghuzziyyah* We crossed the mountain and reached a Turkic tribe known as the Ghuzziyyah. Much to our surprise,[17] we discovered that they are nomads who live in animal-hair tents that they pitch and strike regularly. Their tents were pitched with some in one place and the same number in another place, as is the practice of transhumant nomads. They lead wretched lives. They are like roaming asses.[18] They practice no recognizable form of monotheism, they do not base their beliefs on reason, and they worship nothing—indeed they call their own chiefs "lord."[19] When one of them consults his chief on a matter, he says to him, "My lord, what shall I do about such and such?" «They decide matters by consultation»,[20] though it is quite possible for the lowliest and most worthless individual in their community to turn up and overturn the consensus they have reached. To be sure, I have heard them declare, "There is no god but God! Muḥammad is God's emissary." But this was a way of ingratiating themselves with the Muslims passing through their lands and not out of conviction. When one of them is wronged or something unpleasant happens to him, he raises his head to the heavens and shouts, "Bīr Tankrī," which in Turkic means "By God, by the One!" *Bīr* means "one" and *Tankrī* is "God" in the language of the Turks. They do not clean themselves when they defecate or urinate, and they do not wash themselves when intercourse puts them in a state of ritual impurity. They avoid contact with water, especially in the winter.

19 Their womenfolk do not cover themselves in the presence of a man, whether he be one of their menfolk or not. A woman will not cover any part of her body in front of anyone, no matter who. One day we stopped at a tent and sat down. The man's wife sat with us. During conversation, she suddenly uncovered her vulva and scratched it, right in front of us. We covered our faces and exclaimed, "God forgive us!" but her husband simply laughed and said to the

interpreter,[21] "Tell them: we might uncover it in your presence and you might see it, but she keeps it safe so no one can get to it. This is better than her covering it up and letting others have access to it." Illicit intercourse is unheard of. If they catch anyone attempting it in any way, they tear him in half, in the following manner: they join the branches of two trees, tie the culprit to the branches and then let the trees loose. The man tied to the trees is torn in two.

One of them heard me reciting the Qur'an and found it beautiful. 20
He approached the interpreter and said, "Tell him not to stop." One day, this man said to me via the interpreter, "Ask this Arab, 'Does our great and glorious Lord have a wife?'" I was shocked by his words, praised God and asked His forgiveness. He copied my actions. Such is the custom of the Turk—whenever he hears a Muslim declare God's glory and attest His uniqueness, he copies him.

Their marriage customs are as follows. One man asks another for 21
one of his womenfolk, be it his daughter, sister, or any other woman he possesses, in exchange for such and such a number of Khwārazmī garments. When he is paid in full, he hands her over. Sometimes the dowry is in camels, horses, or the like. The man is not granted access to his future wife until he has paid the full dowry that he has agreed with her guardian. Once paid, he shows up unabashedly, enters her dwelling, and takes possession of her right there and then, in the presence of her father, mother, and brothers. No one stops him.

When one of them dies and leaves a wife and sons behind, the 22
eldest son marries his dead father's wife, provided she is not his birth mother. No one, merchant or anyone else for that matter, can perform a ritual wash in their presence, except at night when he will not be seen, because they get very angry. They exact payment from him and exclaim, "This man has planted something in the water[22] and wants to put a spell on us!"

No Muslim can pass through their territory without first 23
befriending one of them. He lodges with him and brings gifts from the Muslim lands: a roll of cloth, a headscarf for his wife, pepper, millet, raisins, and nuts. When he arrives, his friend pitches a

yurt for him and provides him with sheep, in accordance with his status. In this way, the Muslim can perform the ritual slaughter, as the Turks do not do this but instead beat the sheep on the head until it dies. If someone has decided to travel and uses some of the camels and horses belonging to his friend the Turk, or if he borrows some money, his debt with his friend remains unpaid. He takes the camels, horses, and money he needs from his friend. On his return, he pays the Turk his money and returns his camels and horses.[23] So too, if someone a Turk doesn't know passes through and says, "I am your guest. I want some of your camels, horses, and dirhams," he gives him what he asks for. If the merchant dies on the trip and the caravan returns, the Turk comes to meet the caravan and says, "Where is my guest?" If they say, "He is dead," he brings the caravan to a halt, goes up to the most eminent merchant he sees, unties his goods as the merchant looks on, and takes the exact number of dirhams he had advanced to the first merchant, not a penny more. He also takes back the exact number of camels and horses, saying, "He was your cousin, so you are under the greatest obligation to pay his debt." If the guest runs away, he behaves in the same way, only this time he says, "He was a Muslim like you. You get it back from him." If he does not meet his Muslim guest on the road, he asks three men about him, saying, "Where is he?" When told where he is, he travels, even for days, till he finds him and reclaims his property, along with the gifts he gave him. The Turk also behaves like this when he travels to al-Jurjāniyyah. He asks for his guest and stays with him until he leaves. If the Turk dies while staying with his Muslim friend and the Muslim later passes through this territory as a member of a caravan, they put him to death, with the words, "You imprisoned him and killed him. Had you not imprisoned him, he would not have died." Likewise, they kill the Muslim if he gives the Turk alcohol and he falls and dies. If he does not travel as a member of the caravan, they seize the most important member of the caravan and kill him.

24 They abhor pederasty. A man from Khwārazm lodged with the tribe of the *kūdharkīn* (the deputy of the king of the Turks) and lived

for a while with one of his hosts. He was there to trade in sheep. The Turk had a beardless son, whom the Khwārazmī blandished and tried to seduce[24] until he gave in. The Turk turned up, found the two of them in the act, and brought the matter to the *kūdharkīn*, who said to him, "Muster the Turks," which he did, as was the practice. The *kūdharkīn* said to the Turk, "Do you wish me to rule according to what is true or what is false?" "According to what is true." "Then fetch your son!" The son was fetched. "Both must be put to death together." The Turk was angered and said, "I shall not surrender my son." "Then let the merchant pay a ransom," he said. The Turk paid a number of sheep for what had been done to his son, and four hundred ewes to the *kūdharkīn*, for the punishment that had been averted. Then he left the realm of the Turks.

The first king and chief we met was the Lesser Yināl. He had converted to Islam but had been told that, "If you convert to Islam, you will never lead us," so he recanted. When we arrived at his camp, he said, "I cannot allow you to pass. This is unheard of. It will never happen." We gave him some gifts. He was satisfied with a Jurjānī caftan worth ten dirhams, a cut of woven cloth, some flat breads, a handful of raisins, and a hundred nuts. When we handed them over, he prostrated himself before us. This is their custom: when a person is generous to another, the other prostrates himself before him. He said, "Were our tents not far from the road, we would bring you sheep and grain." He left us and we carried on. 25

The next morning we encountered a solitary Turk—a despicable figure, unkempt and really quite repulsive—a man of no worth at all. It had started to rain heavily. "Halt!" the man said. The entire caravan ground to a halt: it numbered about three thousand mounts and five thousand men. "Not one of you will pass," he said. We obeyed and said, "We are friends of the *kūdharkīn*." He approached and said with a laugh, "*Kūdharkīn* who? Do I not shit on the beard of the *kūdharkīn*?" Then he shouted, "Bakand"—"bread" in the language of Khwārazm—and I gave him some flat breads, which he took, saying, "Proceed. I have spared you out of pity." 26

27 Ibn Faḍlān said: The members of a household do not approach someone who is ill. His slaves, male and female, wait on him. He is put in a tent, away from the other tents, where he remains until he dies or recovers. A slave or a pauper is simply thrown out onto the open plain and left. The Turks dig a large ditch, in the shape of a chamber for their dead. They fetch the deceased, clothe him in his tunic and girdle, and give him his bow.[25] They put a wooden cup filled with alcohol in his hand and place a wooden vessel of alcohol in front of him. They bring all his wealth and lay it beside him, in the chamber. They put him in a sitting position and then build the roof. On top they construct what looks like a yurt made of clay. Horses are fetched, depending on how many he owned. They can slaughter any number of horses, from a single horse up to a hundred or two. They eat the horse meat, except for the head, legs, hide, and tail, which they nail to pieces of wood, saying, "His horses which he rides to the Garden."[26] If he has shown great bravery and killed someone, they carve wooden images, as many as the men he has killed, place them on top of his grave and say, "His retainers who serve him in the Garden." Sometimes they do not kill the horses for a day or two. Then an elder will exhort them: "I have seen So-and-So," (i.e., the deceased) "in a dream and he said to me, 'You see me here in front of you. My companions have gone before me. My feet are cracked from following them. I cannot catch up with them. I am left here, all alone.'" Then they bring his horses, slaughter them, and gibbet them at his graveside. A day or two later, the elder arrives and says, "I have seen So-and-So. He said, 'Inform my household and companions that I have caught up with those who[27] went before me and have recovered from my exhaustion.'"

28 Ibn Faḍlān said: Each and every one of the Turks plucks his beard but does not touch his mustache. I would often see one of their aged elders, clad in a sheepskin, his beard plucked but with a little left under his chin. If you caught sight of him from a distance, you would be convinced he was a billy goat.

The king of the Ghuzziyyah Turks is called *yabghū*. This is the title given to the ruler of the tribe and is their name for their emir. His deputy is called *kūdharkīn*. Any one who deputizes for a chief is called *kūdharkīn*. 29

Upon leaving the region where this group of Turks was camped, we stopped with their field marshal, Atrak, son of al-Qaṭaghān. Turkish yurts were pitched, and we were lodged in them. He had a large retinue with many dependents, and his tents were big. He gave us sheep and horses: sheep for slaughter and horses for riding. He summoned his paternal cousins and members of his household, held a banquet and killed many sheep. We had presented him with a gift of clothing, along with raisins, nuts, pepper, and millet.[28] I watched his wife, who had previously been the wife of his father,[29] take some meat, milk, and a few of the gifts we had presented and go out into the open, where she dug a hole and buried everything, uttering some words. "What is she saying?" I asked the interpreter, and he replied, "She says, 'This is a gift for al-Qaṭaghān, the father of Atrak. The Arabs gave it to him.'" 30

That night the interpreter and I were granted an audience in Atrak's yurt. We delivered the letter from Nadhīr al-Ḥaramī, instructing him to embrace Islam. The letter specifically mentioned that he was to receive fifty dinars (some of them *musayyabīs*), three measures of musk, some tanned hides, and two rolls of Marw cloth. Out of this we had cut for him two tunics, a pair of leather boots, a garment of silk brocade, and five silk garments. We presented his gift and gave his wife a headscarf and a signet ring. I read out the letter and he told the interpreter, "I will not respond until you have returned. Then I shall inform the caliph of my decision in writing." He removed the silk shirt he was wearing and put on the robe of honor we have just mentioned. I noticed that the tunic underneath was so filthy that it had fallen to pieces. It is their custom not to remove the garment next to their body until it falls off in tatters. 31

He had plucked all of his beard and mustache, so he looked like a eunuch. Even so, I heard the Turks state that he was their most 32 accomplished horseman. In fact, I was with him one day, on horseback. A goose flew past. I saw him string his bow, move his horse into position under the bird, and fire. He shot the goose dead.

33 One day he summoned the four commanders of the adjacent territory: Ṭarkhān, Yināl, the nephew of Ṭarkhān and Yināl, and Yilghiz. Ṭarkhān was blind and lame and had a withered arm, but he was by far the most eminent and important. Atrak said, "These are the envoys from the king of the Arabs to my son-in-law, Almish, son of Shilkī. I cannot rightfully allow them to go any further without consulting you." Ṭarkhān said, "Never before have we seen or heard of a thing like this. Never before has an envoy from the caliph passed through our realm, even when our fathers were alive. I suspect that it is the caliph's design to send these men to the Khazars and mobilize them against us. Our only option is to dismember these envoys and take what they have." Someone else said, "No. We should take what they have and let them go back naked where they came from." Another said, "No. We should use them as ransom for our fellow tribesmen taken prisoner by the king of the Khazars." They debated like this for seven long days. We were in the jaws of death. Then, as is their wont, they came to a unanimous decision: they would allow us to continue on our way. We presented Ṭarkhān with a robe of honor: a Marw caftan and two cuts of woven cloth. We gave a tunic to his companions, including Yināl. We also gave them pepper, millet, and flat breads as gifts. Then they left.

34 We pushed on as far as the Bghndī River, where the people got their camel-hide rafts out, spread them flat, put the round saddle frames from their Turkish camels inside the hides, and stretched them tight. They loaded them with clothes and goods. When the rafts were full, groups of people, four, five, and six strong, sat on top of them, took hold of pieces of *khadhank* and used them as oars. The rafts floated on the water, spinning round and round, while the people paddled furiously. We crossed the river in this manner. The horses and the camels were urged on with shouts, and they swam across. We needed to send a group of fully armed

soldiers across the river first, before the rest of the caravan. They were the advance guard, protection for the people against the Bāshghird. There was a fear they might carry out an ambush during the crossing. This is how we crossed the Bghndī River. Then we crossed a river called the Jām, also on rafts, then the Jākhsh, the Adhl, the Ardn, the Wārsh, the Akhtī, and the Wbnā. These are all mighty rivers.

Then we reached the Bajanāk. They were encamped beside a still lake as big as a sea. They are a vivid brown color, shave their beards, and live in miserable poverty, unlike the Ghuzziyyah. I saw some Ghuzziyyah who owned ten thousand horses and a hundred thousand head of sheep. The sheep graze mostly on what lies underneath the snow, digging for the grass with their hooves. If they do not find grass, they eat the snow instead and grow inordinately fat. During the summer, when they can eat grass, they become very thin.[30] 35

The Bajanāk

We spent a day with the Bajanāk, continued on our way, and stopped beside the Jaykh River. This was the biggest and mightiest river we had seen and had the strongest current. I saw a raft capsize in the river and all the passengers on board drown. A great many died, and several camels and horses drowned, too. It took the greatest effort to get across. Several days' march later, we crossed the Jākhā, the Azkhn, the Bājāʿ, the Smwr, the Knāl, the Sūḥ, and the Kījlū. 36

We stopped in the territory of a tribe of Turks called the Bāshghird. We were on high alert, for they are the wickedest, filthiest, and most ferocious of the Turks. When they attack, they take no prisoners. In single combat they slice open your head and make off with it. They shave their beards. They eat lice by carefully picking over the hems of their tunics and cracking the lice with their teeth. Our group was joined by a Bāshghird who had converted to Islam. He used to wait on us. I saw him take a louse he found in his clothing, crack it with his fingernail, and then lick it. "Yum!" he said, when he saw me watching him. 37

The Bāshghird

38 Each carves a piece of wood into an object the size and shape of a phallus and hangs it round his neck. When they want to travel or take the field against the enemy, they kiss it and bow down before it, saying, "My lord, do such and such with me." I said to the interpreter, "Ask one of them to explain this. Why does he worship it as his lord?" "Because I came from something like it and I acknowledge no other creator," he replied. Some of them claim that they have twelve lords: a lord for winter, a lord for summer, a lord for rain, a lord for wind, a lord for trees, a lord for people, a lord for horses, a lord for water, a lord for night, a lord for day, a lord for death, a lord for the earth. The lord in the sky is the greatest, but he acts consensually, and each lord approves of the actions of his partners. «God is exalted above what the wrongdoers say!»[31] We noticed that one clan worships snakes, another fish, and another cranes. They told me that they had once been routed in battle. Then the cranes cried out behind them, and the enemy took fright, turned tail, and fled, even though they had routed the Bāshghird. They said, "These are his actions: he has routed our enemies." This is why they worship cranes. We left their territory and crossed the following rivers: the Jrmsān, the Ūrn, the Ūrm, the Bāynāj, the Wtīʿ, the Bnāsnh, and the Jāwshīn.[32] It is about two, three, or four days travel from one river to the next.

39 *The Bulghārs* We were a day and night's march away from our goal. The king of the Ṣaqālibah dispatched his brothers, his sons, and the four kings under his control to welcome us with bread, meat, and millet. They formed our escort. When we were two *farsakh*s away, he came to meet us in person. On seeing us, he got down from his horse and prostrated himself abjectly, expressing thanks to the great and glorious God! He had some dirhams in his sleeve and showered them over us. He had yurts pitched for us, and we were lodged in them. We arrived on Sunday the twelfth of Muharram, 310 [May 12, 922]. We had been on the road for seventy days since leaving al-Jurjāniyyah.[33] From Sunday to Wednesday we

remained in our yurts, while he mustered his kings, commanders, and subjects to listen to the reading of the letter.

When they had gathered on the Thursday, we unfurled the two standards we had brought with us, saddled the horse with the saddle meant for the king, dressed him in black, and placed a turban on his head. I brought out the letter of the caliph and said, "We are not permitted to remain seated during the reading of the letter." He stood up, as did the chiefs in attendance. He was big and corpulent. I read the beginning of the letter, and, when I reached the phrase, "Peace be upon you! On your behalf, I praise God—there is no god but Him!" I said, "Return the greetings of the Commander of the Faithful." They did so, without exception. The interpreter translated everything, word by word. When we had finished the letter, they shouted "God Almighty!" at the top of their voices. The ground under our feet shook. 40

I next read the letter of the vizier Ḥāmid ibn al-ʿAbbās. The king continued to stand. I told him to be seated, so he sat down for the reading of the letter of Nadhīr al-Ḥaramī. When I had finished, his companions showered him with many dirhams. Then I produced the gifts meant for him and his wife: unguents,[34] clothes, and pearls. I presented one gift after another until I had handed over everything. Then, in front of his people, I presented a robe of honor to his wife, who was seated by his side. This is their customary practice. The womenfolk showered dirhams on her after I had presented the robe. Then we left. 41

An hour later, he sent for us, and we were shown into his tent. The kings were on his right. He ordered us to sit on his left. His sons were seated in front of him. He sat alone, on a throne draped in Byzantine silk. He called for the table. It was carried in, laden with roasted meat and nothing else. He picked up a knife, cut off a piece of meat, and ate it, then a second piece and a third, before anyone else. Then he cut off a piece and handed it to Sawsan, the envoy, who had a small table placed in front of him in order to receive it. Such is their custom. No one reaches for the food before the king 42 hands him a portion and a table is provided for him to receive it—the moment he receives it, he gets a table. He handed me a piece next, and I was given a table. He handed a piece to the fourth king, and he was given a table.[35] Then he handed some meat to his sons, and they were given tables. Each of us ate from the table intended for his sole use. No one took anything from any other table. When the king was done with the food, everyone took what remained on his own table back to his lodging.

43 After the meat, he called for the honey drink *sujū*, which he drinks night and day,[36] and drank a cupful. Then he stood up and said, "Such is my joy in my patron the Commander of the Faithful, may God prolong his life!" The four kings and his sons stood up when he did. So did we. When he had done this three times, we were shown out.

44 Before I turned up, the phrase "Lord God, keep in piety the king Yilṭawār, king of the Bulghārs!"[37] was proclaimed from the *minbar* during the Friday oration. I told the king, "God is the king, and He alone is to be accorded this title from the *minbar*. Great and glorious is He! Take your patron, the Commander of the Faithful. He is satisfied with the phrase, 'Lord God, keep in piety the imam Jaʿfar al-Muqtadir bi-llāh, your humble servant, caliph, and Commander of the Faithful!' This is proclaimed from his *minbar*s east and west. His forefathers, the caliphs before him, did the same. The Prophet (God bless and cherish him!) said, 'Do not exaggerate my importance the way the Christians exaggerate the importance of Jesus, the son of Mary, for I am simply ʿAbdallāh: God's bondsman and His emissary.'"[38] He asked me, "What proclamation can I rightly use for the Friday oration?" and I said, "Your name and that of your father." "But my father was an unbeliever," he said, "and I do not wish to have his name mentioned from the *minbar*. Indeed, I do not wish to have even my own name mentioned, because it was given me by an unbeliever. What is the name of my patron, the Commander of the Faithful?" "Jaʿfar," I replied. "Am I permitted to take his name?" "Yes." "Then I take Jaʿfar as my name, and ʿAbdallāh as the name

of my father. Convey this to the preacher." I did so. The proclamation during the Friday oration became, "Lord God, keep in piety Your bondsman Jaʿfar ibn ʿAbdallāh, the emir of the Bulghārs, whose patron is the Commander of the Faithful!"

Three days after I had read out the epistle and presented the gifts, he summoned me. He had learned of the four thousand dinars and of the subterfuge employed by the Christian in order to delay their payment.[39] The dinars had been mentioned in the letter. When I was shown in, he commanded me to be seated. I sat down. He threw the letter from the Commander of the Faithful at me. "Who brought this letter?" "I did." Then he threw the vizier's letter at me. "And this one?" "I did," I replied. "What has been done," he asked, "with the money they refer to?" "It could not be collected. Time was short, and we were afraid of missing the crossing. We left the money behind, to follow later." "You have all arrived," he said. "My patron has given you this sum to be brought to to me, so I can use it to build a fort to protect myself against the Jews who have reduced me to slavery. My man could have brought me the gifts." "Indeed he could have. We did our best." Then he said to the interpreter, "Tell him that I do not acknowledge any of the others. I acknowledge only you. They are not Arabs. If my master (God give him support!) thought that they could have read the official letter as eloquently as you, he would not have sent you to keep it safe for me, read it, and hear my response. I do not expect to receive one single dirham from anyone but you. Produce the money. This would be the best thing for you to do."[40] I left the audience, dazed and in a state of terror. I was overawed by his demeanor. He was a big, corpulent man, and his voice seemed to come from inside a barrel. I left the audience, gathered my companions, and told them about our conversation. "I warned you about this," I said.[41] 45

At the start of the prayer, his muezzin would repeat the phrases announcing the start of prayer twice.[42] I said to him, "These phrases are announced only once in the realm of your patron the Commander of the Faithful." So he told the muezzin, "Accept what he 46 tells you and do not contravene him." The muezzin performed the call to prayer as I had suggested for several days. During this time the king would interrogate me and argue about the money. I would try to persuade him to give up his hopes and explained our reasons. When he despaired of receiving the money, he instructed the muezzin to revert to a repeated announcement. The muezzin did so. The king meant it as a pretext for debate. When I heard the muezzin announce the start of prayer twice, I shouted to him to stop. The muezzin informed the king. The king summoned me and my companions.

47 He said to the interpreter, "Ask him (he meant me), what is his opinion on two muezzins, one of whom announces the call once, the other twice, both of whom lead the people in prayer? Is the prayer permissible or not?" "The prayer is permissible," I said. "Is there any disagreement on this, or is there consensus?" "There is consensus," I said. "Ask him, what is his opinion about someone who has given to one group of people a sum of money intended for another group of people, weak people, sorely beset and reduced to slavery, betrayed by the first group?" "This is impermissible," I replied, "and they are wicked people." "Is there any disagreement, or is there consensus?" "There is consensus," I said. Then he said to the interpreter, "Ask him, do you think that if the caliph—God give him long life!—were to send an army against me he would be able to overpower me?" "No," I answered. "What about the emir of Khurasan, then?" "No." "Is it not because we are separated by vast distance and many infidel tribes?" he asked. "Of course," I answered. "Tell him, by God—here I am, in this far-off land where we are now, you and I both, yet still I fear my patron the Commander of the Faithful. I fear his curse, should he learn anything displeasing about me. I would die on the spot, though his kingdom is a great distance away. Yet you who eat his bread, wear his clothes, and look on him constantly have betrayed him in the matter of a letter he commanded you to bring to me, to my weak people. You have betrayed the Muslims. I shall accept no instruction from you on how to practice my

religion until a sincere counselor arrives. I will accept instruction from such a man." He had dumbfounded us—we had no answer. We left. Ibn Faḍlān said: From then on, he would show me favor and be affable towards me, addressing me as Abū Bakr the Veracious.[43] But he was aloof from my companions.

48 I lost count of the number of marvels I witnessed in his realm. For example, on our first night in his territory, at what I reckoned was about an hour before sunset,[44] I saw the horizon turn a bright red. The air was filled with a mighty uproar, and I heard the din of many voices. I looked up and was surprised to see fiery-red clouds close by. Loud voices came from the clouds, where there were shapes that looked like soldiers and horses. These shapes brandished swords and spears. I could form a clear image of them in my mind. Then another group, similar to the first, appeared. I could make out men, animals, and weapons. This second group charged the first, one squadron attacking the other. We were scared and began to pray to God and entreat Him. The locals were astonished at our reaction and laughed at us. Ibn Faḍlān said: We watched as one unit charged the other, engaged in combat for an hour and then separated. After an hour they disappeared. We asked the king about this, and he told us that his forebears used to say, "These are two groups of jinn, believers and unbelievers, who do battle every evening." He added that this spectacle had occurred every night for as long as they could remember.

49 Ibn Faḍlān said: I went into my yurt with the king's tailor, a man from Baghdad who had ended up there. We were chatting but did not chat for long—less time than it takes you to read halfway through one seventh of the Qur'an.[45] It was beginning to grow dark, and we were waiting for the call to prayer at nightfall. When we heard it we went outside the yurt and noticed that the morning sun had already arisen. So I said to the muezzin, "Which prayer did you call?" "The daybreak prayer." "And what about the last call, the night call?" "We perform that along with the sunset prayer." So I said, "And what of the night?" "The nights are as short as you observed.

They have been even shorter but now they have started to grow long." He said that he had not slept for a month, afraid he would miss the morning prayer. You can put a cooking-pot on the fire at the time of the sunset prayer, and by the time you have performed the morning prayer, the pot will not have started to boil. Daylight was very long. I observed that, for part of the year, the days were long and the nights short. Later on I observed the nights grow long and the days short.[46]

50 On our second night, I sat down outside the yurt and watched the sky. I could make out only a few constellations, I think about fifteen. I noticed that the red glow that precedes sunset did not disappear—night was hardly dark at all. In fact you could identify another person at more than a bow-shot away. The moon did not reach the middle of the sky. It would rise in one part of the sky for an hour, then dawn would break, and the moon would set. The king told me that a tribe called the Wīsū lived three months from his territory, where night lasted less than an hour. Ibn Faḍlān said: I noticed that, at sunrise, the whole country, the ground, the mountains, anything you cared to look at, grew red. The sun rose like a giant cloud. The red persisted until the sun was at its zenith. The inhabitants of Bulghār informed me, "In winter, night is as long as day is now and day is as short as night. If we set out at sunrise for a place called Itil less than a *farsakh* away, we will not get there before nightfall, when all the constellations have risen and cover the sky." When we left Bulghār territory, night had grown long and day short.[47]

51 They consider the howling of dogs to be very auspicious, I observed. They rejoice and say, "A year of fertility, auspiciousness, and peace." Snakes, I noticed, are so numerous that ten, maybe even more, could be coiled around just one branch of a tree. The Bulghārs do not kill them, and the snakes do not harm them. There was one place where I saw a felled tree more than one hundred cubits in length. I noticed that it had a very thick trunk, so I stopped to examine it. All of a sudden it moved. I was terrified. When I looked

closely, I noticed a snake of almost the same length and bulk lying on top of it. When it saw me, it slid off the trunk and disappeared among the trees. I left in a state of alarm and told the king and his companions, but they were unimpressed. The king said, "Have no fear. It will do you no harm."

When we were traveling in the company of the king, we halted at 52
a place where my comrades Takīn, Sawsan, Bārs, one of the King's companions, and I entered a copse. We saw a small piece of dark wood, slender as the staff of a spindle, though a bit longer, with a dark shoot. A broad leaf from the top of the shoot spread on the ground. What looked like berry-bearing calyxes were scattered on it. You could easily mistake the taste of these berries for sweet seedless pomegranates. We ate them, and they were delicious. We spent the rest of our time there looking for them and eating them.

The apples, I noticed, are dark. In fact, they are extremely dark 53
and more acidic than wine vinegar. The female slaves eat them, and they get their name from them.[48] Hazel trees grow in abundance. I saw hazel woods everywhere. One wood can measure forty by forty *farsakh*s. There is another tree that grows there, but I don't know what it is. It is extremely tall, has a leafless trunk, and tops like the tops of palm trees, with slender fronds, but bunched together. The locals know where to make a hole in the trunk. They place a container underneath it. Sap, sweeter than honey, flows from the hole. If someone drinks too much sap, he gets as intoxicated as he would from drinking wine.

Their diet consists chiefly of millet and horse meat, though 54
wheat and barley are plentiful. Crop-growers keep what they grow for themselves. The king has no right to the crops, but every year they pay him one sable skin per household. When he orders a raid on a given territory, he takes a share of the booty they bring back. For every wedding feast or banquet the king is given a jug of honey wine, some wheat (of very poor quality, because the soil is black and so foul-smelling), and a gift of food. The amount of food depends on the size of the banquet.

55 They have nowhere to store their food, so they dig holes in the ground as deep as wells to store it. It only takes a few days for it to rot and give off such an odor that it becomes inedible. They do not use olive oil, sesame oil, or any other vegetable oil. They use fish oil instead. Everything they prepare in it is unwholesome and greasy. They make a broth from barley and give it to slaves of both sexes. Sometimes they cook the barley with some meat. The owners eat the meat, and feed the female slaves the barley, unless the broth is made with the head of a goat, in which case the female slaves are given the meat.

56 They wear peaked caps. The king rides out alone, unaccompanied by his men or anyone else. If he passes through the market, everyone stands, removes his cap from his head, and places it under his arm. When the king has passed, they put their caps back on. The same is true of those who are given an audience with the king, the great and the lowly—even his sons and his brothers. The moment they are in his presence, they remove their caps and place them under their arms. Then they bow their heads, sit down, and stand up again, until he commands them to be seated. Those who sit in his presence, do so in a kneeling position. They keep their hats under their arms until they have left. Then they put them back on again.

57 They live in yurts. The king's yurt is enormous and can hold more than a thousand people. It is carpeted with Armenian rugs. In the middle the king has a throne bedecked with Byzantine silk.

58 One of their customs is for the grandfather, rather than the father, to pick up a new-born boy and declare, "It is my right to care for him and raise him to manhood. It is not the father's right to do so." The brother, not the son, inherits the estate of a deceased man. I told the king that this was impermissible, and I taught him clearly how the inheritance laws work. He understood them.

59 I observed more lightning there than anywhere else. They do not approach a household struck by lightning but let it be, with all of its

contents, people, and possessions—everything, in fact—until time destroys it. They say, "This household has incurred divine wrath."

They impose capital punishment upon anyone who kills on purpose. For manslaughter, they make a box out of *khadhank*, put the perpetrator inside and nail it fast. They give him three loaves of bread and a flagon of water, erect three pieces of wood in the shape of the frame of a camel saddle and suspend him inside, saying, "We set him between heaven and earth, exposed to the rain and the sun. Perhaps God will have pity on him." He remains there until his body rots over time and is scattered to the winds. 60

If they notice that someone is clever and able, they say, "This man is fit for the service of our lord." They take hold of him, place a rope around his neck and hang him from a tree until he decomposes. The king's interpreter told me that a man from Sind turned up once and served him for a while. This man was clever and able. A group of Bulghārs decided to go on one of their journeys. The man from Sind asked the king's permission to accompany them, but he refused. The man persisted until the king relented and gave his permission. So the man set sail with them. They noticed that he was quick-witted and clever and conspired as follows: "This man is fit for the service of our lord. Let us send him to him." Their route took them past a forest, so they took hold of the man, placed a rope around his neck, tied it to the top of a big tree, and left him there. Then they went on their way. 61

If one of them urinates on a march while still in full armor, everything he has with him, weapons and clothes, is removed as plunder. This is one of their customs. But they leave him alone if he undoes his weapons and puts them aside while urinating. 62

Men and women wash naked together in the river without covering themselves, and yet under no circumstance do they commit adultery. When they catch an adulterer, they set four rods in the ground and tie his hands and his feet to them, no matter who he may be. Then they take an axe, and cut him up, from neck to thigh. 63

They treat the woman in the same manner. They hang the pieces from a tree. I spared no effort to exhort the women to cover themselves in the presence of the men, but that proved impossible. They kill a thief in the same way as they kill an adulterer.

64 There are bees in the woods, and honey is abundant. They know where the bees are to be found and gather the honey. Sometimes they are surprised by an enemy tribe who kills them.

65 Many merchants live there. They travel to the territory of the Turks and bring back sheep and travel to another land, called Wīsū, and bring back sable and black fox.

66 There was one household of five thousand individuals, men and women. They had all converted to Islam and are known as the Baranjār. They had built a mosque out of wood to pray in but did not know how to read the Qur'an. I taught one group how to conduct their prayers. A man named Saul converted to Islam under my supervision, and I gave him the name ʿAbdallāh, but he said, "I want you to give me your name—Muḥammad." I did so. His wife, mother, and children also converted. They all took the name Muḥammad.[49] I taught him the suras «Praise be to God» and «Say, He is God, One.»[50] He took greater delight in these suras than if he had been made king of the Ṣaqālibah.

67 We first encountered the king in an encampment at Khljh, a group of three unfathomable[51] lakes, two large, one small. It was about a *farsakh* away from a large river called the Itil, which they used and which flowed to the realm of the Khazars. On the bank of this river there is a market, open from time to time, where many valuable goods are sold.[52]

68 Takīn had told me that a giant lived in the king's territory. When I arrived, I asked the king about this, and he replied, "Yes, he used to live among us, but he died. He was not one of the local inhabitants—in fact, he was not really human. This is his story. A group of merchants went to the Itil, one day away, as is their custom. Now, this river was in spate and had burst its banks. Barely a day later a group of merchants came back and said, 'Your Majesty, there is a

man who has followed the course of the river. If he is from a community close by, then we cannot remain in our homes. We will have to migrate.' So I rode to the river with them. I was surprised by what I found when I got there—a man twelve cubits tall, using my forearm as a measure, with a head the size of a huge cooking-pot, a nose more than a span in length, two great eyes, and fingers longer than a span. He unnerved me, and I was gripped by the very terror that had gripped the others. We tried to speak to him, but he did not answer. He just looked at us. So I had him brought to my residence and wrote to the inhabitants of Wīsū, three months distant, asking them for information. They wrote back: 'He is one of the Gog and Magog, who live three months away from us in a state of absolute nakedness. The sea separates us. They live on the far side of the sea, on its shore. They mate with one another, like the beasts of the field. Every day the great and glorious God provides them with a fish from the sea. They come one by one with their knives and cut as much as they need to feed them and their dependents. If they take more than they need, they develop a pain in their stomach. Their dependents also develop a pain in their stomachs. Should he die, then they all die too. When they have what they need from the fish, it flips over and is taken back into the sea. This is how they live day by day. On one side we are separated from them by the sea. They are hemmed in by mountains on all other sides. A wall separates them from the gate from which they will swarm forth.[53] When almighty God intends them to swarm forth into the inhabited lands, He will cause the wall to be breached, the sea will dry up, and the fish will no longer be provided.'"[54] I asked the king about the man. He said, "He stayed with me for a while, but any boys who looked at him died, and pregnant women miscarried. His hands would crush to death anyone he took hold of. When I saw this happening, I hanged him from a tall tree and killed him. If you want to see his bones and skull, I will take you." "By God, I would like that very much," I said. So we rode out to a great wood, and he led me to a tree where the man's bones and skull had fallen. His head was like a bees' nest, and the bones of his ribs, legs, and forearms were larger than the boughs of a palm tree. I departed, filled with wonder.

69 Ibn Faḍlān said: The king traveled from Khljh to a river called Jāwshīr, where he stayed for two months. When he was ready to leave, he sent a message to a people called Suwāz and commanded them to travel with him. They refused and split into two groups. One sided with his son-in-law W*rʿ, who had become their king. The king sent them a message: "Almighty God has given me the gift of Islam and granted me membership in the kingdom of the Commander of the Faithful. I am His bondsman. He has made me his emir. I will wage war on those who oppose me." The other group aligned themselves with the king of the Askil tribe, who was under the king's sovereignty, though he had not accepted Islam. When the king of the Bulghārs sent the Suwāz this epistle, they were afraid he might attack, so they joined him in his journey to the Jāwshīr river. This is not a very wide river—it is no more than five cubits wide, but the water reaches a man's navel, and comes up to his collar-bone in some places. At its deepest point, it reaches the height of a man. It is surrounded by many trees,[55] including *khadhank* trees.

70 There is a wide plain near the river, where they say an animal smaller than a camel but larger than a bull lives. It has the head of a camel, the tail and hooves of a bull, and the body of a mule. It has a single, round, thick horn in the middle of its head. As the horn grows it becomes narrow and resembles a spearhead. Some of these animals are five cubits tall, some three, with a degree of variation. It eats succulent and tasty leaves from the trees. It charges any horseman it sees. A fleet mare will just about escape, with some effort. But if the animal overtakes the horseman, it unseats him from his horse and tosses him in the air with its horn. Then it rushes him with its horn again and again and kills him, though it pays no heed whatsoever to the horse. They hunt it to death on the plain and in the woods. They climb the tall trees in the wood where the animal lives, and a group of archers with poisoned arrows work together.

When the animal is in their midst they shoot it, exhaust it, and kill it. In the king's tent I saw three large bowls that looked as if they were made of Yemeni onyx. The king informed me that they were made out of the base of this animal's horn. Some of the locals claim that this animal is the rhinoceros.

Ibn Faḍlān said: I saw no one in ruddy health. Most of them are sickly, and the majority regularly die from the colic. Even the child at the breast suffers from it. When a Muslim dies and a woman from Khwārazm is present,[56] they wash the body as the Muslims do and then bear him on a cart, preceded by a standard, until they come to his grave. Then they take him from the cart and place him on the ground, draw a line around him, and remove him. They dig his grave, build his tomb, and bury him inside the line they have drawn. This is their burial custom. The women do not weep for the deceased, the men do. They arrive on the day of his death, stand at the entrance to his yurt, and howl and weep in the ugliest and wildest way. And these are freeborn men! When they have finished weeping, the slaves of the deceased bring leather thongs. The men continue to mourn and beat their flanks and exposed parts of their bodies with the leather thongs, leaving weals like those left by the lashes of a whip. At the entrance to his yurt they are required to erect a standard, bring his weapons, and place them around his grave. They weep for two years and then take the standard down and cut off their hair. The deceased's relatives hold a banquet to indicate that they have emerged from mourning. The deceased's wife, if he had one, then takes a husband. Such is their custom for their chieftains. Ordinary folk do not do as much as this for their dead. 71

The king of the Ṣaqālibah is obliged to pay to the king of the Khazars a tribute of one sable skin for every tent in his kingdom. When the boat from Khazar territory reaches Ṣaqālibah territory, the king goes on board and counts its contents, taking a tenth of its cargo. When the Rūs or any other people come with slaves, the king of the Ṣaqālibah has the right to choose one in every ten. The king of the Khazars holds the son of the king of the Ṣaqālibah as a hostage.[57] 72

The king of the Khazars heard that the daughter of the king of the Ṣaqālibah was beautiful, so he asked for her hand in marriage but was refused. He sent some troops and took her by force, though he is a Jew and she a Muslim. She died at his court, so he demanded a second daughter. As soon as the king of the Ṣaqālibah heard this, he was afraid that the king of the Khazars might take her by force, as he had her sister, so he married her to the king of the Askil, who recognizes his authority.[58] It was fear of the king of the Khazars that forced the king of the Ṣaqālibah to write to the caliph and petition him to build him a fortress.

73 Ibn Faḍlān said: I asked him the following question one day and said, "You have an extensive kingdom, many belongings, and considerable wealth from taxes. Why did you petition the caliph for an unspecified sum of money to build a fortress?" He replied, "I could see that the realm of Islam was flourishing and that the wealth of the Muslims was acquired lawfully. That is why I asked for it. If I had wanted to build a fort using my own silver and gold, I could have. I wanted the money of the Commander of the Faithful to bring me blessings, so I sent him my petition."

The Rūsiyyah

74 Ibn Faḍlān said: I also saw the Rūsiyyah. They had come to trade and had disembarked at the Itil River. I have never seen bodies as nearly perfect as theirs. As tall as palm trees, fair and reddish, they wear neither tunics nor caftans. Every man wears a cloak with which he covers half of his body, so that one arm is uncovered. They carry axes, swords, and daggers and always have them to hand. They use Frankish swords with broad, ridged blades. They are dark from the tips of their toes right up to their necks—trees, pictures, and the like.[59]

75 Every woman wears a small box made of iron, silver, brass, or gold, depending on her husband's financial worth and social standing, tied at her breasts. The box has a ring to which a knife is attached, also tied at her breasts.[60] The women wear neck rings of gold and silver. When a man has amassed ten thousand dirhams,

he has a neck ring made for his wife. When he has amassed twenty thousand dirhams, he has two neck rings made. For every subsequent ten thousand, he gives a neck ring to his wife. This means a woman can wear many neck rings. The jewelry they prize the most is the dark ceramic beads they have aboard their boats and which they trade among themselves. They purchase beads for one dirham each and string them together as necklaces for their wives.

They are the filthiest of all God's creatures. They have no mod- 76
esty when it comes to defecating or urinating and do not wash themselves when intercourse puts them in a state of ritual impurity. They do not even wash their hands after eating. Indeed, they are like roaming asses.[61] They arrive, moor their boats by the Itil, and build large wooden houses on its banks. They share a house, in groups of ten and twenty, sometimes more, sometimes fewer. Each reclines on a couch. They are accompanied by beautiful female slaves for trade with the merchants. They have intercourse with their female slaves in full view of their companions. Sometimes they gather in a group and do this in front of each other. A merchant may come in to buy a female slave and stumble upon the owner having intercourse. The Rūs does not leave her alone until he has satisfied his urge. They must wash their faces and their heads each day with the filthiest and most polluted water you can imagine.[62] Let me explain. Every morning a female slave brings a large basin full of water and hands it to her master. He washes his hands, face, and hair in the water. Then he dips the comb in the water and combs his hair. Then he blows his nose and spits in the basin. He is prepared to do any filthy, impure act in the water. When he has finished, the female slave carries the basin to the man next to him who performs the same routine as his comrade. She carries it from one man to the next and goes around to everyone in the house. Every man blows his nose and spits in the basin, and then washes his face and hair.

They disembark as soon as their boats dock. Each carries bread, 77
meat, onions, milk, and alcohol to a large block of wood set in the ground. The piece of wood has a face on it, like the face of a man.

It is surrounded by small figurines placed in front of large blocks of wood set in the ground. He prostrates himself before the large figure and says, "Lord, I have come from a distant land, with such and such a number of female slaves and such and such a number of sable pelts." He lists all his merchandise. Then he says, "And I have brought this offering." He leaves his offering in front of the piece of wood, saying, "I want you to bless me with a rich merchant with many dinars and dirhams who will buy from me whatever I wish and not haggle over any price I set." Then he leaves. If he finds it hard to sell his goods and has to stay there too many days, he comes back with a second and a third offering. If his wishes are not fulfilled, he brings an offering to every single figurine and seeks its intercession, saying, "These are the wives, daughters, and sons of our lord." He goes up to each figurine in turn and petitions it, begging for its intercession and groveling before it. Sometimes business is good, and he makes a quick sale. In that case, he says, "My lord has satisfied my request, so I need to compensate him." He acquires some sheep or cows and kills them, gives a portion of the meat as alms, and places the rest before the large block of wood and the small ones around it. He ties the heads of the cows or the sheep to the piece of wood set up in the ground. When night falls, the dogs come and eat it all up, and the man who has gone to all this trouble says, "My lord is pleased with me and has eaten my offering."

78 When one of them falls ill, they pitch a tent far away and lay him down inside, with some bread and water. They do not approach him or speak to him. Indeed, they have no contact with him for as long as he is ill, especially if he is a social inferior or a slave. If he recovers and gets back on his feet, he rejoins them. If he dies, they set fire to him. They do not bury dead slaves but leave them as food for the dogs and the birds.

79 When they catch a thief or a bandit, they take him to a solid tree and put a sturdy rope around his neck. They tie him to the tree and he hangs there until he eventually decomposes from exposure to the rain and the winds.

I was told that they set fire to their chieftains when they die. Sometimes they do more,[63] so I was very keen to verify this. Then I learned of the death of an important man. They had placed him in his grave, with a roof raised over him, for ten days while they finished cutting and sewing his garments. When the deceased is poor, they build a small boat for him, place him inside and burn it. When he is rich, they collect his possessions and divide them into three portions. One-third goes to his household, one-third is spent on his funeral garments, and one-third is spent on the alcohol they drink the day his female slave kills herself and is cremated with her master. They are addicted to alcohol. They drink it night and day. Sometimes one of them dies cup in hand. When the chieftain dies, the members of his household ask his female and male slaves, "Who will die with him?" One answers, "I will." At this point the words become binding. There is no turning back. It is not even an option. It is usually the female slaves who offer. 80

When the man I just mentioned died, they said to his female slaves, "Who will die with him?" One said, "I will." So they put two other female slaves in charge of her, caring for her and accompanying her wherever she went, even to the point of washing her feet with their hands. Then they attended to the chieftain, cutting his garments and setting in order what was required for him. The female slave drank alcohol every day and sang merrily and cheerfully. 81

I arrived at the river where his boat was moored on the day the chief and the female slave were set on fire. I noticed that the boat had been beached and that it was supported by four *khadhank* props. These props were surrounded by what looked like huge structures of wood. The boat had been hauled on top of the wood. The Rūsiyyah approached, going to and fro around the boat uttering words I did not understand. The chief was still in his grave and had not been exhumed. They produced a couch and placed it on the boat, covering it with quilts and cushions made of Byzantine silk brocade. An aged woman whom they called the Angel of Death turned up. She spread the coverings on the couch. It is her responsibility to sew 82 the chieftain's garments and prepare him properly, and it is she who kills the female slaves. I saw her myself: she was gloomy and corpulent but neither young nor old.[64]

83 When they arrived at his grave, they removed the soil from the wood. Then they removed the wood and exhumed him, dressed in the garment he was wearing when he died. I noticed that the coldness of the climate had turned him black. They had placed alcohol, fruit, and a *ṭanbūr* in his grave. They removed all of this. Surprisingly, his corpse had not begun to stink. Only his color had deteriorated. They dressed him in trousers, leggings, boots, a tunic, and a silk caftan with gold buttons. They placed a peaked silk cap fringed with sable on his head. They carried him inside the yurt that was on the ship and rested him on a quilt, propping him up with the cushions. They placed the alcohol, fruit, and basil beside him. Then they placed bread, meat, and onions in front of him. They cut a dog in two and threw it onto the boat. They placed all his weaponry beside him. They made two horses gallop into a sweat, cut them into pieces with a sword, and threw the meat onto the boat. They cut two cows into pieces and threw them on board. Then they produced a cock and a hen, killed them, and put them on board too.

84 Meanwhile, the female slave who had expressed her wish to die came and went, entering one yurt after another. The owner of the yurt would have intercourse with her and say, "Tell your master that I have done this out of love for you." At the time of the Friday late afternoon prayer they brought the female slave to an object they had built that resembled a door-frame. She stood on the hands of the men and rose like the sun above the door-frame. She uttered some words, and they brought her down. They lifted her up a second time, and she did what she had done before. They lowered her and lifted her a third time, and she did what she had done the last two times. Then they handed her a hen. She cut off the head and cast it aside. They picked the hen up and threw it onto the boat. I quizzed the interpreter about her actions and he said, "The first time they lifted her up, she said, 'Look, I see my father and

mother.' The second time she said, 'Look, I see all my dead kindred, seated.' The third time she said, 'Look, I see my master, seated in the Garden.[65] The Garden is beautiful and dark-green. He is with his men and his retainers. He summons me. Go to him.'" They took her to the boat and she removed both of her bracelets, handing them to the woman called the Angel of Death, the one who would kill her. She also removed two anklets she was wearing, handing them to the two female slaves who had waited upon her, the daughters of the woman known as the Angel of Death.

They lifted her onto the boat but did not take her into the yurt. 85
The men approached with shields and sticks and handed her a cup of alcohol. Before drinking it she chanted over it. The interpreter said to me, "Now she bids her female companions farewell." She was handed another cup which she took and chanted for a long time. The crone urged her to drink it and to enter the yurt where her master was lying. I could see she was befuddled. She went to enter the yurt but missed it, placing her head to one side of the yurt, between it and the boat. The crone took hold of her head and entered the yurt with her. The men began to bang their shields with the sticks, so that the sound of her screaming would be drowned out. Otherwise, it would terrify the other female slaves, and they would not seek to die with their masters.

Six men entered the yurt. They all had intercourse with the 86
female slave and then laid her beside her master. Two held her feet, two her hands. The crone called the Angel of Death placed a rope around her neck with the ends crossing one another and handed it to two of the men to pull on. She advanced with a broad-bladed dagger and began to thrust it in between her ribs, here and there, while the two men strangled her with the rope until she died.

The deceased's nearest male relative came forward. He picked 87
up a piece of wood and set it alight. He was completely naked. He walked backwards, the nape of his neck towards the boat, his face towards the people. He had the ignited piece of wood in one hand and had his other hand on his anus. He set fire to the wooden

structures under the boat. The people came forward with sticks and firewood. They each carried a lighted stick that they threw on top of the wood. The wood caught fire. Then the boat, the yurt, the dead man, the female slave, and everything else on board caught fire. A fearsome wind picked up. The flames grew higher and higher and blazed fiercely.

88 One of the Rūsiyyah was standing beside me. I heard him speaking to the interpreter who was with me. I asked him what he had said, and he replied, "He said, 'You Arabs, you are a lot of fools!'" "Why is that?" "Because you purposefully take your nearest and dearest and those whom you hold in the highest esteem and put them in the ground, where they are eaten by vermin and worms. We, on the other hand, cremate them there and then, so that they enter the Garden on the spot." I asked about this and he said, "My lord feels such great love for him that he has sent the wind to take him away within an hour." In fact, it took scarcely an hour for the boat, the firewood, the female slave, and her master to be burnt to ash and then to very fine ash. The Rūsiyyah then built a structure like a round hillock over the beached boat, and placed a large piece of *khadhank* in the middle. They wrote the man's name and the name of the king of the Rūsiyyah on it. Then they left.

89 Ibn Faḍlān said: It is one of the customs of the king of the Rūsiyyah to keep in his palace four hundred of his bravest comrades and most trusted companions beside him. They die when he dies and sacrifice themselves to protect him. Each one has a female slave to wait on him, wash his head, and provide him with food and drink, and a second to have intercourse with. These four hundred companions sit below his huge couch, studded with precious stones. Forty concubines who belong to the king also sit on his couch. Sometimes he has intercourse with one of them in the presence of his comrades. He never steps off his throne. When he wants to satisfy an urge, he does so in a salver. When he wants to ride, he has his horse brought to the throne and mounts it from there. When he wants to dismount, he rides the horse to the throne so he can dismount

there. He has a deputy, who leads the armies, fights the enemy, and represents him among his subjects.

The title of the king of the Khazars is *khāqān.* He appears in public only once every four months, at a distance. He is called the Great Khāqān. His deputy is called Khāqān Bih, who leads and commands the army, manages and conducts the affairs of the kingdom, and appears in public and leads the raids. The neighboring kings obey him.[66] He enters 90

The Khazars

Yāqūt's Quotations From The Book of Ibn Faḍlān

Itil[67]

... I read the following in the written account of Aḥmad ibn Faḍlān ibn al-ʿAbbās ibn Rāshid ibn Ḥammād, the envoy of al-Muqtadir to the realm of the Ṣaqālibah (i.e., the people of Bulghār): Y1.1

[68] I learned that a giant lived there. When I arrived, I asked the king about this, and he replied, "Yes, he used to live among us, but he died. He was not one of the local inhabitants—in fact, he was not really human. This is his story. A group of merchants went to the Itil, one day away, as is their custom. Now, this river was in spate and had burst its banks. Barely a day later a group of merchants came back and said, 'Your Majesty, there is a man who has followed the course of the river. If he is from a community close by, then we cannot remain in our homes. We will have to migrate.' So I rode to the river with them. I was surprised by what I found when I got there—a man twelve cubits tall, using my forearm as a measure, with a head the size of a huge cooking-pot, a nose more than a span in length, two great eyes, and fingers longer than a span. He unnerved me, and I was gripped by the very terror that had gripped the others. We tried to speak to him, but he did not answer. He just looked at us. So I had him brought to my residence and wrote to the inhabitants of Wīsū, three months distant, asking them for information. They wrote back: 'He is one of the Gog and Magog, who live three months away from us in a state of absolute nakedness. The Y1.2

sea separates us. They live on the far side of the sea, on its shore. They mate with one another, like the beasts of the field. Every day the great and glorious God provides them with a fish from the sea. They come one by one with their knives and cut as much as they need to feed them and their dependents. If they take more than they need, they develop a pain in their stomach. Their dependents also develop a pain in their stomachs. Should he die, then they all die, too. When they have what they need from the fish, it flips over and is taken back into the sea. This is how they live day by day. On one side we are separated from them by the sea. They are hemmed in by mountains on all other sides. A wall separates them from the gate from which they will swarm forth. When Almighty God intends them to swarm forth into the inhabited lands, He will cause the wall to be breached, the sea will dry up, and the fish will no longer be provided.'" The king said, "He stayed with me for a while, but he developed an illness in his chest that proved terminal." I went to see his bones. They filled me with great fear.

Y1.3 May Almighty God have mercy on the author. I take no responsibility for this and similar statements he makes. I give no guarantee of their accuracy. Ibn Faḍlān's tale of how al-Muqtadir sent him to Bulghār is still preserved. It is well known and popular with people. I saw many copies of it.

Bāshghird[68]

Y2.1 . . . The king of the Ṣaqālibah and the people of his realm had converted to Islam. The Commander of the Faithful, al-Muqtadir bi-llāh, sent Aḥmad ibn Faḍlān ibn al-ʿAbbās ibn Rāshid ibn Ḥammād as his envoy to bestow on the king a robe of honor and teach him the rules of Islam, according to the sharia. Al-Muqtadir was Ibn Faḍlān's patron. Muḥammad ibn Sulaymān was also Ibn Faḍlan's patron. Ibn Faḍlān left a description of all his experiences from the time of his departure from Baghdad, in the month of Safar, 309 [June, 921], until the time of his return. He wrote the following as part of his account of the Bāshghird:

[37] We stopped in the territory of a tribe of Turks called the Bāshghird. We were on high alert, for they are the wickedest, most powerful, and most ferocious of the Turks. When they attack they take no prisoners. In single combat they chop off your head and make off with it. They shave their beards. They eat lice by carefully picking over the hems of their tunics and cracking the lice with their teeth. Our group was joined by a Bāshghird who had converted to Islam. He used to wait on us. I saw him take a louse he found in his clothing, crack it with his fingernail and then lick it. "Yum!" he said when he saw I was watching him. [38] Each carves a piece of wood into an object the size and shape of a diadem and hangs it round his neck. When they want to travel or take the field against the enemy, they kiss it and bow down before it, saying, "My lord, do such and such with me." I said to the interpreter, "Ask one of them to explain this. Why does he worship it as his lord?" "Because I came from something like it. I acknowledge this alone as the giver of life," he replied. Some of them claim that they have twelve lords: a lord for winter, a lord for summer, a lord for rain, a lord for wind, a lord for trees, a lord for people, a lord for horses, a lord for water, a lord for night, a lord for day, a lord for death, a lord for life, and a lord for the earth.[69] The lord in the sky is the greatest, but he acts consensually, and each lord approves of the actions of his partners. God is exalted above what the wrongdoers and the repudiators say![70] Ibn Faḍlān said: We noticed that one clan worships snakes, another fish, and another cranes. They told me that they had once been routed in battle. Then the cranes cried out behind them, and the enemy took fright, turned tail, and fled, even though they had routed the Bāshghird. They said, "These are our lord, because they have routed our enemies." This is why they worship cranes. Y 2.2

This is what he says they said. Y 2.3

Bulghār[71]

. . . The king of Bulghār and his subjects had converted to Islam during the reign of al-Muqtadir bi-llāh. They sent an envoy to Y 3.1

Baghdad to inform al-Muqtadir of this and to petition him to send them people to teach them how to perform their prayers correctly and acquaint them with the rules of Islam, according to the sharia. I have not been able to discover the cause of their conversion. I read an epistle that Aḥmad ibn Faḍlān ibn al-ʿAbbās ibn Asad[72] ibn Ḥammād wrote. He was the envoy of al-Muqtadir bi-llāh to the king of the Ṣaqālibah, and his patron was Muḥammad ibn Sulaymān. In the epistle he gave an account of all his experiences, from his departure from Baghdad until his return. He said:

Y 3.2 [2] When the letter of Almis, son of Shilkī Bilṭawār the king of the Ṣaqālibah, was delivered to al-Muqtadir bi-llāh, the Commander of the Faithful, the king petitioned the caliph to send people to instruct him in law and acquaint him with the rules of Islam according to the sharia, to construct a mosque and build a *minbar* from which he could proclaim al-Muqtadir's name throughout his kingdom. He also beseeched him to build a fort to protect him against the kings who opposed him. His requests were granted. [3] The representative of the king of the Ṣaqālibah at court was Nadhīr al-Ḥaramī. I, Aḥmad ibn Faḍlān, began by reading al-Muqtadir's letter to the king, presenting him with the official gifts designated, and supervising the jurists and instructors. The caliph's envoy was Sawsan al-Rassī. Sawsan's patron was Nadhīr al-Ḥaramī. We traveled from Baghdad, City of Peace, on Thursday the twelfth of Safar, 309 [June 21, 921].

Y 3.3 Ibn Faḍlān proceeds to record everything that occurred on the road to Khwārazm and then on the road from Khwārazm to the realm of the Ṣaqālibah. It would take too long to quote it and comment on it. Ibn Faḍlān said:

Y 3.4 [39] We were a day and night's march from our goal. The king of the Ṣaqālibah dispatched his brothers, his sons, and the four kings under his control to welcome us with bread, meat, and millet. They formed our escort. When we were two *farsakh*s away, he came to meet us in person. On seeing us, he got down from his horse and prostrated himself abjectly, expressing thanks to God! He had some dirhams in his sleeve and showered them over us. He had yurts pitched for us, and we were lodged in them. We arrived on Sunday the twelfth of Muharram, 310 [May 12, 922]. We had been on the road for seventy days since leaving al-Jurjāniyyah, the main city of Khwārazm. We remained in our yurts through Wednesday, while the kings and the elite of the realm gathered to listen to the reading of the letter. [40] On Thursday we unfurled the two standards we had brought with us, saddled the horse with the saddle meant for the king, dressed him in black, and placed a turban on his head. I brought out the letter of the caliph and read it while he stood. [41] I next read the letter of the vizier Ḥāmid ibn al-ʿAbbās. The king continued to stand. He was a big man. His companions showered him with many dirhams. Then we produced the gifts and presented them and then presented a robe of honor to his wife, who was seated by his side. This is their customary practice. [42] Later he sent for us, and we attended him in his tent. The kings were on his right. He ordered us to sit on his left. His sons were seated in front of him. He sat alone, on a throne draped in Byzantine silk. He called for the table. It was carried in, laden with roasted meat. He picked up a knife, cut off a piece of meat, and ate it, then a second piece and a third, before anyone else. Then he cut off a piece and handed it to Sawsan, the envoy, who had a small table placed in front of him in order to receive it. Such is their custom. No one reaches for the food before the king hands him a portion and a table is provided for him to receive it—the moment he receives it, he gets a table. He cut off a piece and handed it to the king on his right and he was given a table. He handed some meat to the second king and he was given a table. This continued until everyone present was given a table. Each of us ate from the table intended for his sole use. No one took anything from any other table. When the meal was finished, everyone took what remained on his own table back to his lodging. [43] When we had finished, he called for the honey drink they call *sujū* and drank, as did we.

[44] Before we turned up, the phrase "Lord God, keep in piety the king Yilṭawār, king of the Bulghārs!" was proclaimed from Y3.5

the *minbar* during the Friday oration. I told the king, "God is the king, and He alone is to be accorded this title, especially from the *minbar*. Take your patron, the Commander of the Faithful. He has given instructions that the phrase, 'Lord God, keep in piety the imam Jaʿfar al-Muqtadir bi-llāh, your humble servant, caliph and Commander of the Faithful!' be proclaimed from his *minbar*s east and west." He asked me, "What proclamation can I rightly use for the Friday oration?" and I said, "Your name and that of your father." "But my father was an unbeliever," he said, "and I do not wish to have his name mentioned from the *minbar*. Indeed I do not wish to have even my own name mentioned, because it was given me by an unbeliever. What is the name of my patron, the Commander of the Faithful?" "Jaʿfar," I replied. "Am I permitted to take his name?" "Yes." "Then I take Jaʿfar as my name, and ʿAbdallāh as the name of my father." This was conveyed to the preacher. The proclamation during the Friday oration became, "Lord God, keep in piety Your bondsman Jaʿfar ibn ʿAbd Allāh, the emir of Bulghārs, whose patron is the Commander of the Faithful!"

Y 3.6 Ibn Faḍlān said: [48] I lost count of the number of marvels I witnessed in his realm. For example, on our first night in his territory, an hour before sunset, I saw the horizon turn a bright red. The air was filled with an uproar and loud voices. I looked up and was surprised to see fiery-red clouds nearby. The voices and the uproar came from the clouds, where there were shapes that looked like soldiers and horses. These shapes brandished bows, spears, and swords. I could form a clear image of them in my mind. Then another group, similar to the first, appeared. I could make out men, animals, and weapons. This second group charged the first, as one squadron attacks another. We were scared and began to pray to God and entreat Him. The locals were astonished at our reaction and laughed at us. Ibn Faḍlān said: We watched as one unit charged the other, engaged in combat for an hour, and then separated. This lasted for a part of the night, then they disappeared. We asked the king about this, and he told us that his forebears used to say, "These are two groups of jinn, believers and unbelievers, who do battle every evening." This spectacle had occurred every night for as long as they could remember.

[49] Ibn Faḍlān said: I went into my yurt with the king's tailor, a man from Baghdad. We were chatting but did not chat for long—less than half an hour, I reckon. We were waiting for the call to prayer at nightfall. When we heard it, we went outside the yurt, and noticed that the morning sun had already risen. So I said to the muezzin, "Which prayer did you call?" "The daybreak prayer." "And what about the last call, the night call?" "We perform that along with the sunset prayer." So I said, "And what of the night?" "The nights are as short as you have observed. They have been even shorter but now they have started to grow long." He said that he had not slept for a month, afraid he would miss the morning prayer. You can put a cooking pot on the fire at the time of the sunset prayer, and by the time you have performed the morning prayer, the pot will not have started to boil. Ibn Faḍlān said: Daylight was very long. I observed that, for part of the year, the days were long and the nights short. Later on I observed the nights grow long and the days short. [50] On our second night, I sat down outside and could make out only a few constellations, I think maybe no more than fifteen. I noticed that the red glow that precedes sunset did not disappear—night was hardly dark at all. In fact you could identify another person at more than a bow-shot away. Ibn Faḍlān said: The moon would rise in one part of the sky for an hour, then dawn would break, and the moon would set. The king told me that a tribe called the Wīsū lived three months from his territory, where night lasted less than an hour. Ibn Faḍlān said: I noticed that at sunrise the whole country, the ground, the mountains, anything you cared to look at, grew red. The sun rose like a giant cloud. The red persisted until the sun was at its zenith. The inhabitants of Bulghār informed me, "In winter, night is as long as day is now and day is as short as night. If we set out at sunrise for a place called Itil less than a *farsakh* away, we will not get there before nightfall, when all the constellations have risen and cover the sky." Y 3.7

Y 3.8 [51] They consider the howling of a dog to be very auspicious, I observed. They say that a year of fertility, auspiciousness, and peace approaches. Snakes, I noticed, are so numerous that ten, maybe even more, could be coiled around just one branch of a tree. The Bulghārs do not kill them, and the snakes do them no harm. [53] The apples are dark. In fact, they are extremely dark and more acidic than wine vinegar. The female slaves eat them and get fat. Hazel trees grow in abundance. I saw hazel woods everywhere. One wood can measure forty by forty *farsakhs*. There is another tree that grows there, but I don't know what it is. It is extremely tall, has a leafless trunk, and tops like the tops of palm trees, with slender fronds, but bunched together. The locals know where to make a hole in the trunk. They place a container underneath it. Sap, sweeter than honey, flows from the hole. If someone drinks too much sap, he gets as intoxicated as he would from drinking wine. [54] Their diet consists chiefly of millet and horse meat, though wheat and barley are plentiful. Crop-growers keep what they grow for themselves. The king has no right over the crops, but every year they pay him one ox skin per household. When he orders a raid on a given territory he takes a share of the booty they bring back. [55] They do not use olive oil, sesame oil, or any other vegetable oil. They use fish oil instead. This is why they are so greasy. [56] They wear peaked caps. The king rides out alone, unaccompanied by his men or anyone else. If he passes through the market, everyone stands, removes his cap from his head and places it under his arm. When the king has passed, they put their caps back on. The same is true of those who are given an audience with the king, the great and the lowly—even his sons and his brothers. The moment they are in his presence, they remove their caps and place them under their arms. Then they bow their heads, sit down, and stand up again until he commands them to be seated. Those who sit in his presence, do so in a kneeling position. They keep their hats under their arms until they have left. Then they put them back on again.

[59] I observed more lightning there than anywhere else. They do not approach a household struck by lightning but let it be with all of its contents, people, and possessions—everything in fact—until time destroys it. They say, "This household has incurred divine wrath." [61] If they notice that someone is clever and able, they say, "This man is fit for the service of our lord." They take hold of him, place a rope around his neck, and hang him from a tree until he decomposes. [62] If one of them urinates on a march while still in full armor, everything he has with him, including his weapons, is removed as plunder. But they leave him alone if he undoes his weapons and puts them aside while urinating. This is one of their customs. [63] Men and women wash naked together in the river without covering themselves, and yet under no circumstance do they commit adultery. When they catch an adulterer, they set four rods in the ground and tie his hands and his feet to them, no matter who he may be. Then they take an axe, and cut him up, from neck to thigh. They treat the woman in the same manner. They hang the pieces from a tree. Ibn Faḍlān said: I spared no effort to exhort the women to cover themselves when swimming in the presence of men, but that proved impossible. They kill a thief in the same way they do an adulterer. Y3.9

Aḥmad ibn Faḍlān gives many more items of information about the Bulghār but we have confined ourselves to this. Y3.10

Khazar[73]

... Aḥmad ibn Faḍlān was the envoy of al-Muqtadir bi-llāh to the king of the Ṣaqālibah. In an epistle in which he gave an account of all his experiences in these regions he said: Y4.1

Khazar is the name of a clime containing a fortified town called Itil. Itil is the name of the river that flows to Khazar from al-Rūs and Bulghār. Itil is a city. Khazar is the name of the kingdom, not the name of a city. Itil has two parts. One part, the bigger of the two, is on the west bank of the Itil. The other is on the east. The king, called *yilik* and also *bāk* in their tongue, lives on the west bank. Y4.2

The western part of the city stretches for about a *farsakh* and is surrounded by a wall. The wall has a flat top for patrols. They use felt tents for buildings, apart from a few clay structures. They have markets and baths. Many Muslims live there—more than ten thousand, it is said—and there are around thirty mosques. The king's palace, made of brick, is far from the river bank. This is their only brick building as the king will permit no one else to build with brick. The wall has four gates, one by the river, another by the steppe behind the city. The king is a Jew and, it is said, boasts a retinue of four thousand men. The Khazar population is Muslim and Christian with a number of idolaters. The Jews are the minority sect, though the king is a Jew. Muslims and Christians are the majority. The king and his elite are Jews. In their customs and practices, they live predominantly as the idolaters do—each bows down before the other in order to demonstrate reverence. The various customs of the Muslims, Jews, and Christians determine the rules that govern their township. The king's army is made up of twelve thousand men. This number never decreases: a dead man is replaced immediately. They have no regular stipend, apart from a pittance that they receive, to cover long periods when they go to war or are mustered to deal with an emergency. The various kinds of wealth acquired by the Khazars derive from tolls and their custom of tithing the goods that arrive by road, river, and sea. They also impose a duty on the inhabitants of the neighboring trading emporia and surrounding areas. This duty can take any form, including food and drink and other requirements. The king has nine judges: Jews, Christians, Muslims, and idolaters. They rule on cases that need deciding, and they, not the litigants, communicate with the king. When the court is in session, the judges send their inquiries to the king via a representative. This is how they make contact with him. He delivers his verdict and they implement it.

Y4.3 There are no villages in the countryside around the city. The fields produce their crops without being regularly tended. In the summer they travel about twenty *farsakh*s out into the fields and work the land. They harvest the crops when the crops reach the river and the steppes and transport them by cart and boat. Their staples are rice and fish and other foodstuffs exported to them from al-Rūs, Bulghār, and Kūyābah. The eastern half of the Khazar city is inhabited largely by merchants and Muslims. This is where trading takes place. The language of the Khazars is not similar to Turkic and Persian. It is unique among spoken languages. The Khazars do not resemble the Turks. They have black hair and are of two kinds. One kind, called the Qarākhazar,[74] is brown. They get their name from their deep brown, almost black, coloration and look like Indians. The other kind is fair-skinned, beautiful, and comely. Slavery is practiced among the Khazars, but only the idolaters engage in it, as they permit the buying and selling of their children and enslaving one another. It is contrary to the religious beliefs of the Jews and the Christians, as it is of the Muslims, to enslave a co-religionist. No product is exported from the Khazar realm. Anything acquired there (flour, honey, wax, silk, or skins, for example) is imported.

[90] The title of the king of the Khazars is *khāqān*. He only Y 4.4
appears in public once every four months, at a distance. He is called the Great Khāqān. His deputy is called Khāqān Bih, who leads and commands the army, manages and conducts the affairs of the kingdom, appears in public and leads the raids. The neighboring kings obey him. He enters[75] the presence of the Great Khāqān every day, abasing himself in a show of humility and meekness. He must enter his presence barefoot, with a piece of firewood in his hand. When he greets him, he lights the firewood in front of him, and then sits on the couch with the king at his right hand. He is represented by a man called Kundur Khāqān, who in turn is represented by a man called Jāwashīghar.[76] According to custom, the Great Khāqān does not sit before the people or speak to them. Only those functionaries we have mentioned are admitted into his presence. Executive power, the meting out of punishment, and the general management of the kingdom are the responsibility of the deputy, Khāqān Bih. It is the custom that, when the Great Khāqān dies, a large dwelling

is constructed for him. It houses twenty tents,[77] in each of which a grave is dug. Stones are pound to a kohl-like powder and spread on the ground. Lime is thrown on top. A second river flows under both the dwelling and the river—a fast, powerful river. They[78] construct the grave above the river, saying, "This way no devil, man, worm, or vermin can reach him!" Those who bury him in his grave are beheaded, so no one knows which tent houses his grave. His grave is called the Garden, and they say, "He has entered the Garden." All of the tents are carpeted with silk woven with gold. It is the custom of the king of the Khazars to possess twenty-five women, daughters of the neighboring kings, taken either with their compliance or by force.[79] He has sixty concubines, slaves beautiful beyond compare. The freeborn women and the concubines live in a separate palace. Each has a chamber with a vault of teak paneling and surrounded by a pavilion. Each concubine is served by a eunuch as her chamberlain. When the king wants to have intercourse, he sends for the eunuch who places the woman in the king's bed in the blink of an eye. The eunuch stands by the door of the king's yurt. When the king is done with her, the eunuch takes her by the hand and departs. He does not leave her there for one minute longer. When this great king goes out riding, the entire army rides with him. There is a mile between him and his retinue. When his subjects see him, they lie down on their faces and remain prostrate before him. They do not lift their heads until he has passed. His kingship lasts forty years. When it is just one day past forty he is put to death by his subjects, including the elite, who say, "His mind is defective and his judgment is impaired." No squadron he dispatches will turn back or retreat, no matter what. Those who come back after a defeat are killed. If his generals and the deputy are defeated, he has them brought into his presence, along with their women and children, and gives the women and children to another man before their very eyes. He does the same with their horses, belongings, weapons, and residences. Sometimes he cuts them in two and gibbets them. Sometimes he hangs them by the neck from a tree. Sometimes he makes them stable-hands—if he means to be kind to them, that is.

The king of the Khazars has a mighty city on both banks of the Itil. The Muslims are on one bank, the king and his retinue on the other. One of the king's men, a Muslim whose title is Khaz, is in charge of the Muslims. The legal rulings of all the Muslims, both those who reside in the realm of the Khazars and those who go there regularly to trade, are referred to this Muslim retainer. No one else looks into their affairs or judges among them. The Muslims have a congregational mosque in this city. This is where they perform the prayer and gather on Friday, the day of congregation. It has a tall minaret and a number of muezzins. In the year 310 [922–23],[80] the king of the Khazars was informed that the Muslims had razed the synagogue in Dār al-Bābūnj. He gave orders for the minaret to be razed and for the muezzins to be killed. He said: "I would not have razed the mosque, were I not afraid that every synagogue in the territory of Islam would be razed!" The Khazars and their king are Jews. The Ṣaqālibah and those who live on the Khazar border are under his rule. He addresses them as slaves and they owe him their obedience. Some claim that the Khazars are the tribes of Gog and Magog. Y4.5

Khwārazm[81]

I read the following in the epistle that Aḥmad ibn Faḍlān ibn al-ʿAbbās ibn Rāshid ibn Ḥammād wrote. He was the envoy of al-Muqtadir bi-llāh to the king of the Ṣaqālibah, and his patron was Muḥammad ibn Sulaymān. In this work he gives an account of all his experiences from his departure from Baghdad until his return. After his arrival in Bukhara, he said: Y5.1

We arrived in Bukhara and then left for Khwārazm. We travelled downriver from Khwārazm to al-Jurjāniyyah. The distance, by water, is fifty *farsakh*s. Y5.2

I say: These are his very words but I do not know what exactly he means by Khwārazm, because Khwārazm is incontrovertibly the name of the region. Y5.3

Y 5.4 Ibn Faḍlān said: [9] I noticed that, in Khwārazm, the dirhams are adulterated and should not be accepted, because they are made of lead and brass. They call their dirham a *ṭāzijah*. It weighs four and a half *dānaq*s. The money changers trade in sheep bones, spinning tops, and dirhams. They are the strangest of people in the way they talk and behave. When they talk, they sound just like frogs croaking. At the end of the prayer they disavow the Commander of the Faithful, ʿAlī ibn Abī Ṭālib, God be pleased with him. [10] We stayed several days in al-Jurjāniyyah. The River Jayḥūn froze over completely, from beginning to end. The ice was nineteen spans thick.

Y 5.5 God's poor servant ʿAbdallāh[82] said: This is false. The river freezes to an extent of five spans, no more—and even this is a rare occurrence. Normally it is two or three spans thick. I speak from first hand experience. I quizzed the locals about it too. Maybe Ibn Faḍlān thinks that the whole river freezes over, but this is not so. The surface freezes over while the water flows underneath. The people of Khwārazm make a hole in the ice and draw their drinking water from it. This hole is very rarely more than three spans deep.

Y 5.6 Ibn Faḍlān said: [10] Horses, mules, donkeys, and carts used the river like a road and it did not move—it did not even budge. It stayed like this for three months. We thought the country we were visiting was an «infernally cold»[83] portal to the depths of Hell. When snow fell, it was accompanied by a wild, howling blizzard.

Y 5.7 I said: This is also false. If the winter winds did not abate, people could not live there.

Y 5.8 [11] When people here want to honor each other and be generous they say, "Come to my house so we can talk, for I have a good fire burning." This is when they want to express genuine generosity and affability. However, God the exalted has been kind to them by making firewood plentiful and very cheap: a cart load of *ṭāgh* wood (which is the tamarisk) costs only two local dirhams, and their carts can hold about three thousand *raṭl*s.

Y 5.9 I said: Once again this is false. From my experience of transporting some cotton bales, the maximum load their carts can carry is one thousand *raṭls*. The carts they use are drawn by a single animal, be it an ox, a donkey, or a horse. Of course, it is possible that firewood was this cheap during the author's lifetime, but, when I was there, one hundred *mann* cost three *ruknī* dinars.

[11] Normally, their beggars do not stand outside at the door but go into the house, sit for a while and get warm by the fire. Then they say, "Pakand" meaning "bread." They leave, whether they are given some or not. Y 5.10

I said: I actually observed this custom, though it occurs in the countryside and not the town. Then Ibn Faḍlān describes the severe cold, which I too experienced. The mud on the roads would freeze, and the dust would rise into the air when the roads were used. When the rains came and the temperature rose a little, the roads would revert to mud and the animals would sink into it up to their knees. I once tried to write something down but was unable to because the ink in the pot was frozen, and I had to hold it close to the fire and thaw it. Cups would stick to my lips because they were frozen. Blowing on them to warm them up would do no good. And yet for all this, Khwārazm is a pleasant region. Its people are scholars and legal experts, clever men, and wealthy. It is possible to make a living there, and it is possible for them to cultivate the soil and grow crops. Y 5.11

Rūs[84]

I read the following in the epistle of Aḥmad ibn Faḍlān ibn al-ʿAbbās ibn Rāshid ibn Ḥammād. He was the envoy of al-Muqtadir to the king of the Ṣaqālibah, and his patron was Muḥammad ibn Sulaymān. In the work, he gave an account of everything he witnessed, from his departure from Baghdad until his return. I find his account so astonishing that I quote it as I found it. Ibn Faḍlān said: Y 6.1

[74] I also saw the Rūsiyyah. They had come to trade and had disembarked at the Itil River. I have never seen bodies as nearly perfect as theirs. As tall as palm trees, fair, and reddish, they wear neither tunics nor caftans. Every man wears a cloak with which he covers half of his body and leaves one arm uncovered. They carry swords, Y 6.2

daggers, and axes and always have them to hand. They use Frankish swords with broad, ridged blades. They are dark, from the tips of their toes right up to their necks—trees, pictures, and the like. [75] Every woman wears a small box made of iron, brass, silver, or gold, depending on her husband's financial worth and social standing, tied at her breasts. The box has a ring to which a knife is attached, also tied at her breasts. The women wear neck rings of gold and silver. When a man has amassed ten thousand dirhams, he has a neck ring made for his wife. When he has amassed twenty thousand dirhams, he has two neck rings made. For every subsequent ten thousand, he gives a neck ring to his wife. This means a woman can wear many neck rings. The jewelry they prize the most is the dark ceramic beads they have aboard their boats and which they value very highly. They purchase beads for one dirham each and string them together as necklaces for their wives.

Y 6.3 [76] They are the filthiest of all God's creatures. They have no modesty when it comes to defecating or urinating and do not wash themselves when intercourse puts them in a state of ritual impurity. They do not even wash their hands after eating. Indeed they are like roaming asses.[85] They arrive, moor their boats by the Itil, and build large wooden houses on its banks. They share a house, in groups of ten and twenty, sometimes more, sometimes fewer. Each reclines on a couch. They are accompanied by beautiful female slaves for trade with the merchants. They have intercourse with their female slaves in full view of their companions. Sometimes they gather in a group and do this in front of each other. A merchant may come in to buy a female slave and stumble upon the owner having intercourse. The Rūs does not leave her alone until he has satisfied his urge. They must wash their faces and their heads every day with the filthiest and most polluted water you can imagine. Let me explain. Every morning a female slave brings a large basin full of water and hands it to her master. He washes his face, hands, and hair in the water. Then he dips the comb in the water and combs his hair. Then he blows his nose and spits in the basin. He is prepared to do any filthy, impure act in the water. When he has finished, the female slave carries the basin to the man next to him who performs the same routine as his comrade. She carries it from one man to the next and goes around to everyone in the house. Every man blows his nose and spits in the basin, and then washes his face and hair.

[77] They disembark as soon as their boats dock. Each carries bread, meat, milk, onions, and alcohol to a large block of wood set in the ground. The piece of wood has a face on it, like the face of a man. It is surrounded by small figurines placed in front of large blocks of wood set in the ground. He prostrates himself before the large figure and says, "Lord, I have come from a distant land, with such and such a number of female slaves and such and such a number of sable pelts." He lists all his merchandise. Then he says, "And I have brought this offering." He leaves his offering in front of the piece of wood, saying, "I want you to bless me with a rich merchant with many dinars and dirhams who will buy from me whatever I wish and not haggle over any price I set." Then he leaves. If he finds it hard to sell his goods and has to stay there too many days, he comes back with a second and a third offering. If his wishes are not fulfilled, he brings an offering to every single figurine and seeks its intercession, saying, "These are the wives and daughters of our lord." He goes up to each figurine in turn and petitions it, begging for its intercession and groveling before it. Sometimes business is good, and he makes a quick sale. In that case he says, "My lord has satisfied my request, so I need to compensate him." He acquires some sheep and cows and kills them, gives a portion of the meat as alms, and places the rest before the large block of wood and the small ones around it. He ties the heads of the cows and the sheep to the piece of wood set up in the ground. When night falls, the dogs come and eat it all up, and the man who has gone to all this trouble says, "My lord is pleased with me and has eaten my offering." Y6.4

[78] When one of them falls ill, they pitch a tent far away and lay him down inside, with some bread and water. They do not approach him or speak to him. Indeed, they have no contact with him for as Y6.5

long as he is ill, especially if he is a social inferior or a slave. If he recovers and gets back to his feet, he rejoins them. If he dies, they set fire to him. They do not bury dead slaves but leave them as food for the dogs and the birds. [79] When they catch a thief or a bandit, they take him to a solid tree and put a sturdy rope around his neck. They tie him to the tree, and he hangs there until he eventually decomposes through exposure to the rain and the winds.

Y 6.6 [80] I was told that they set fire to their chieftains when they die. Sometimes they do more, so I was very keen to verify this. Then I learned of the death of an important man. They had placed him in his grave with a roof raised over him, for ten days while they finished cutting and sewing his garments. When the deceased is poor, they build a small boat for him, place him inside, and burn it. When he is rich, they collect his possessions and divide them into three portions. One-third goes to his household, one-third is spent on his funeral garments, and one-third is spent on the alcohol they drink the day his female slave kills herself and is cremated with her master. They are addicted to alcohol. They drink it night and day. Sometimes one of them dies cup in hand. When the chieftain dies, the members of his household ask his female and male slaves, "Who will die with him?" One answers, "I will." At this point the words become binding. There is no turning back. It is not even an option. It is usually female slaves who offer. [81] When the man I just mentioned died, they said to his female slaves, "Who will die with him?" One said, "I will." So they put two other female slaves in charge of her, caring for her and accompanying her wherever she went, even to the point of washing her feet with their hands. Then they attended to the chieftain, cutting his garments and setting in order what was required. The female slave drank alcohol every day and sang merrily and cheerfully.

Y 6.7 [82] I arrived at the river where his boat was moored on the day when the chief and the female slave were set on fire. I noticed that the boat had been beached and that it was supported by four props of *khalanj* and other wood. These props were surrounded by what looked like huge structures of wood. The boat had been hauled on top of the wood. The Rūsiyyah approached, going to and fro around the boat, uttering words I did not understand. The chief was still in his grave and had not been exhumed. They produced a couch and placed it on the boat, covering it with quilts and cushions made of Byzantine silk brocade. An aged woman whom they called the Angel of Death turned up. She spread the coverings on the couch. It is her responsibility to sew the chieftain's garments and prepare him properly, and it is she who kills the female slaves. I saw her myself: she was gloomy and corpulent, but neither young nor old. [83] When they arrived at his grave, they removed the soil from the wood. Then they removed the wood and exhumed him, dressed in the garment he was wearing when he died. I saw that the coldness of the climate had turned him black. They had placed alcohol, fruit, and a *ṭanbūr* in his grave. They removed all of this. Surprisingly, only his color had deteriorated. They dressed him in trousers, leggings, boots, a tunic, and a silk caftan with gold buttons. They placed a peaked silk cap fringed with sable on his head. They carried him inside the yurt which was on the boat and rested him on a quilt, propping him up with the cushions. They placed the alcohol, fruit, and basil beside him. Then they placed bread, meat, and onions in front of him. They cut a dog in two and threw it onto the boat. They placed all his weaponry beside him. They made two horses gallop into a sweat, cut them into pieces with their swords, and threw the meat onto the boat. They cut two cows into pieces and threw them on board. Then they produced a cock and a hen, killed them and put them on board too. [84] Meanwhile, the female slave who was to be killed came and went, entering one yurt after another. One by one the owner of the yurt had intercourse with her and said, "Tell your master that I have done this out of love for you." At the time of the Friday late afternoon prayer they brought the female slave to an object they had built that resembled a door-frame. She stood on the hands of the men and she was lifted above the door-frame. She uttered some words, and they brought her down. They lifted her up a second time, and she did what she had done before. They lowered her and lifted her a third time, and she did what she had done the last two times. Then they handed her a hen. She cut off the head and cast it aside. They picked the hen up and threw it onto the boat. I quizzed the interpreter about her actions and he said, "The first time they lifted her up, she said, 'Look, I see my father and mother.' The second time she said, 'Look, I see all my dead kindred, seated.' The third time she said, 'Look, I see my master, seated in the Garden. The Garden is beautiful and dark-green. He is with his men and his retainers. He summons me. Bring me to him.'" They took her to the boat, and she removed both of her bracelets, handing them to the woman called the Angel of Death, the one who would kill her. She also removed two anklets she was wearing, handing them to the two female slaves who had waited upon her, the daughters of the woman known as the Angel of Death. [85] They lifted her onto the boat but did not take her into the yurt. The men approached with shields and sticks and handed her a cup of alcohol. Before drinking it she chanted over it. The interpreter said to me, "Now she bids her female companions farewell." She was handed another cup which she took and chanted for a long time. The crone urged her to drink it and to enter the yurt where her master was lying. I could see she was befuddled. She went to enter the yurt but missed it, placing her head to one side of the yurt, between it and the boat. The crone took hold of her head and entered the yurt with her. The men began to bang their shields with the sticks so that the sound of her screaming would be drowned out. Otherwise it would terrify the other female slaves, and they would not seek to die with their masters. [86] Six men entered the yurt. They all had intercourse with the female slave and then laid her beside her master. Two held her feet, two her hands. The crone called the Angel of Death placed a rope around her neck with the ends crossing one another and handed it to two of the men to pull on. She advanced with a large, broad-bladed dagger and began to thrust it in between her ribs, here and there, while the two men strangled her with the rope until she died.

[87] The deceased's nearest male relative came forward. He picked up a piece of wood and set it alight. He was completely naked. He walked backwards, the nape of his neck towards the boat. He had the ignited piece of wood in one hand and had his other hand on his anus. He set fire to the wooden structure under the boat after they had placed the female slave they had killed next to her master. The people came forward with sticks and firewood. They each carried a lighted stick that they threw on top of the wood. The wood caught fire. Then the boat, the yurt, the dead man, the female slave, and everything else on board caught fire. A fearsome wind picked up. The flames grew higher and higher and blazed fiercely. [88] One of the Rūsiyyah was standing beside me. I heard him speaking to the interpreter who was with him. I asked him what he had said, and he replied, "He said, 'You Arabs, you are a lot of fools! You purposefully take your nearest and dearest and those whom you hold in the highest esteem and put them in the ground, where they are eaten by vermin and worms. We, on the other hand, cremate them there and then, so that they enter the Garden on the spot.'" Then he laughed loud and long and said, "My lord feels such great love for him that he has sent the wind to take him away within an hour." In fact, it took scarcely an hour for the boat, the firewood, the female slave, and her master to be burnt to ash and then very fine ash. The Rūsiyyah then built a structure like a round hillock over the beached boat and placed a large piece of *khadhanj*[86] in the middle. They wrote the man's name and the name of the king of the Rūsiyyah on it. Then they left. Y6.8

[89] Ibn Faḍlān said: it is one of the customs of the kings of the Rūsiyyah to keep in their palaces four hundred of their bravest comrades and most trusted companions beside them. They die when the kings die and sacrifice themselves to protect them. Each companion has a female slave to wait on him, wash his head, and provide him with food and drink, and a second to have intercourse with. These four hundred companions sit below the huge couch of the king, studded with precious stones. Forty concubines who Y6.9

belong to the king also sit on his couch. Sometimes he has intercourse with one of them in the presence of his comrades. He never steps off his throne. When he wants to satisfy an urge, he does so in a salver. When he wants to ride, they bring his horse to the throne, and he mounts it from there. When he wants to dismount, he rides the horse to the throne so he can dismount there. He has a deputy who leads the armies, fights against the enemy, and represents him among his subjects.

Y6.10 I have taken this word for word from Ibn Faḍlān's epistle. He is the one responsible for this account. Only God knows whether it is authentic. Nowadays, everyone knows that the Rūs practice Christianity.

Ibn Faḍlān's Logbook: An Imagined Reconstruction

[4] We traveled from Baghdad, City of Peace, on Thursday, the twelfth of Safar, 309 [June 21, 921]. We stayed one day in Nahrawān, then rode hard until we reached al-Daskarah, where we stayed three days. Then we traveled without delay or diversion and came to Ḥulwān, where we stayed two days. From there we traveled to Qirmīsīn, where we stayed another two days, and next arrived at Hamadhān, where we stayed three days. We traveled to Sāwah and, after two days, on to Rayy, where we stayed eleven days, until Aḥmad ibn ʿAlī, the brother of Ṣuʿlūk, had left Khuwār al-Rayy. Then we traveled to Khuwār al-Rayy itself and three days later to Simnān, then on to al-Dāmghān, where our caravan happened to encounter Ibn Qārin, who was preaching on behalf of the *dāʿī*. We concealed our identity and hurried to Nishapur, where we met Ḥammawayh Kūsā, the field marshal of Khurasan. Līlī ibn Nuʿmān had just been killed. Then we proceeded to Sarakhs, Marw, and Qushmahān, at the edge of the Āmul desert. We stayed three days there and changed camels for the desert journey. We crossed the desert to Āmul and then reached Āfr*n, the outpost of Ṭāhir ibn ʿAlī, on the other side of the Jayḥūn. [5] We traveled via Baykand to Bukhara, where we went straight to al-Jayhānī, the chancellor of the emir of Khurasan, known there as the chief *shaykh*. He had ordered a residence for us and had appointed someone to attend to all our needs and concerns and make sure that we experienced no difficulty in getting what we wanted. After a few days, he arranged an audience with Naṣr ibn Aḥmad. . . . [6] Al-Faḍl ibn Mūsā al-Naṣrānī, Ibn al-Furāt's agent, got wind of this and came up with a plan to deal with Aḥmad ibn Mūsā. He wrote to the deputies of the

superintendent of the Khurasan highway, in the military district of Sarakhs-Baykand. . . . Aḥmad ibn Mūsā was later arrested in Marw and put in chains. We stayed twenty-eight days in Bukhara. [8] . . . We left Bukhara and returned to the river, where we hired a boat for Khwārazm, more than two hundred *farsakhs* from where we hired the boat. We were able to travel only part of the day. A whole day's travel was impossible because of the cold. When we got to Khwārazm, we were given an audience with the emir, Muḥammad ibn ʿIrāq Khwārazm-Shāh. . . . We sailed downriver from Khwārazm to al-Jurjāniyyah. The distance, by water, is fifty *farsakhs*. [10] We stayed several days in al-Jurjāniyyah. The River Jayḥūn froze over completely, from beginning to end. . . . [12] We were in al-Jurjāniyyah for a long time: several days of Rajab, and all of Shaʿban, Ramadan, and Shawwal. . . . [13] Halfway into Shawwal, 309 [February, 922], the season began to change and the river Jayḥūn melted. We set about acquiring the items we needed for our journey. We purchased Turkish camels, constructed the camel-skin rafts for crossing all the rivers we had to cross in the realm of the Turks, and packed provisions of bread, millet, and cured meat to last three months. The locals who knew us told us in no uncertain terms to wear proper clothing and to wear a lot of it. . . . We each wore a tunic, a caftan, a sheepskin, a horse blanket, and a burnoose with only our eyes showing, a pair of trousers, another pair of lined trousers, leggings, and a pair of animal-skin boots with yet another pair on top of them. Mounted on our camels, we wore so many heavy clothes we couldn't move. The jurist, the instructor, and the retainers who had left the City of Peace with us stayed behind, too scared to enter the realm of the Turks. I pushed on with the envoy, his brother-in-law, and the two soldiers Takīn and Bārs. [14] . . . The caravan was ready to depart, so we hired a guide called Falūs, an inhabitant of al-Jurjāniyyah. We trusted in Almighty God and put our fate in His hands. [15] We left al-Jurjāniyyah on Monday, the second of Dhu l-Qaʿdah, 309 [Monday, 4 March, 922], and stopped at an outpost called Zamjān, the Gate of the Turks. The following morning we traveled as far as a stopping post called Jīt. The snow had fallen so heavily that it came up to the camels' knees. We had to stay there two days. Then we kept a straight course and plunged deep into the realm of the Turks through a barren, mountainless desert. We met no one. We crossed for ten days. Our bodies suffered terrible injuries. We were exhausted. The cold was biting, the snowstorms never-ending. It made the cold of Khwārazm seem like summertime. . . . [17] We came to a place where there was a huge quantity of *ṭāgh* wood and stopped. The members of the caravan lit fires and got them going. They took their clothes off and dried them by the fires. Then we departed, traveling as quickly and with as much energy as we could manage, from midnight until the midday or afternoon prayer, when we would stop for a rest. After fifteen nights of this, we came to a huge rocky mountain. Springs of water ran down it and gathered to form a lake at its foot. [18] We crossed the mountain and reached a tribe of the Turks known as the Ghuzziyyah. . . . [25] The first king and chief we met was the Lesser Yināl. . . . We gave him some gifts. He was satisfied with a Jurjānī caftan worth ten dirhams, a cut of woven cloth, some flat breads, a handful of raisins, and a hundred nuts. . . . [30] Upon leaving the region where this group of Turks was camped, we stopped with their field marshal, Atrak, son of al-Qaṭaghān. Turkish yurts were pitched, and we were lodged in them. He had a large retinue with many dependents, and his tents were big. He gave us sheep and horses: sheep for slaughter and horses for riding. He summoned his paternal cousins and members of his household, held a banquet, and killed many sheep. We had presented him with a gift of clothing, along with raisins, nuts, pepper, and millet. [31] That night the interpreter and I were granted an audience in Atrak's yurt. We delivered the letter from Nadhīr al-Ḥaramī, instructing him to embrace Islam. The letter specifically mentioned that he was to receive fifty dinars (some of them *musayyabī*s), three measures of musk, some tanned hides, and two rolls of Marw cloth. Out of this we had cut for him two tunics, a pair of leather boots, a garment of silk brocade, and five silk garments. We presented his gift and gave his wife a headscarf and a signet ring. I read out the letter. . . . [33] One day he summoned the four commanders of the adjacent territory: Ṭarkhān, Yināl, the nephew of Ṭarkhān and Yināl, and Yilghiz. . . . They debated for seven long days. We were in the jaws of death. Then, as is their wont, they came to a unanimous decision: they would allow us to continue on our way. We presented Ṭarkhān with a robe of honor—a Marw caftan and two cuts of woven cloth. We gave a tunic to his companions, including Yināl. We also gave them pepper, millet, and flat breads as gifts. Then they left. [34] We pushed on as far as the Bghndī River, where the people got their camel-hide rafts out, spread them flat, put the round saddle-frames from their Turkish camels inside the hides, and stretched them tight. They loaded them with clothes and goods. When the rafts were full, groups of people, four, five, and six strong, sat on top of them, took hold of pieces of *khadhank* and used them as oars. The rafts floated on the water, spinning round and round, while the people paddled furiously. We crossed the river in this manner. The horses and the camels were urged on with shouts, and they swam across. We needed to send a group of fully armed soldiers across the river first, before the rest of the caravan. They were the advance guard, protection for the people against the Bāshghird. There was a fear they might carry out an ambush during the crossing. This is how we crossed the Bghndī River. Then we crossed a river called the Jām, also on rafts, then the Jākhsh, the Adhl, the Ardn, the Wārsh, the Akhtī, and the Wbnā. These are all mighty rivers. [35] Then we reached the Bajanāk. They were encamped beside a still lake as big as a sea. . . . [36] We spent a day with the Bajanāk, continued on our way, and stopped beside the Jaykh River. This was the biggest and mightiest river we had seen and had the strongest current. I saw a raft capsize in the river and all the passengers on board drown. A great many died, and several camels and horses drowned, too. It took the greatest effort to get across. Several days' march later, we crossed the Jākhā, the Azkhn, the Bājā', the Smwr, the Knāl, the Sūḥ, and the Kījlū. [37] We stopped in the territory of a tribe of Turks called the Bāshghird. . . . [38] . . . We left their territory and crossed the following rivers: the Jrmsān, the Ūrn, the Ūrm, the Bāynāj, the Wtī', the Bnāsnh, and the Jāwshīn. It is about two, three, or four days' travel from one river to the next. [39] We were a day and night's march away from our goal. The king of the Ṣaqālibah dispatched his brothers, his sons, and the four kings under his control to welcome us with bread, meat, and millet. They formed our escort. When we were two *farsakh*s away, he came to meet us in person. On seeing us, he got down from his horse and prostrated himself abjectly, expressing thanks to the great and glorious God! He had some dirhams in his sleeve and showered them over us. He had yurts pitched for us, and we were lodged in them. We arrived on Sunday, the twelfth of Muharram, 310 [May 12, 922]. We had been on the road for seventy days since leaving al-Jurjāniyyah. From Sunday to Wednesday we remained in our yurts, while he mustered his kings, commanders, and subjects to listen to the reading of the letter.

Notes

1 In his entry on the "Bulghār" Yāqūt gives this name as Asad, though his other references to Ibn Faḍlān's full name use Rāshid. Presumably "Asad" is a scribal error.

2 The word *mawlā* that I have translated, in this instance, as "patron" expresses a central feature of Islamic social organization known as *walā'*. The term covers several relationships, including the ownership and manumission of slaves, the patronage of clients, and the protection and support of freeborn men and membership of a person's household. In our text *mawlā* is used to express patronage and clientage, as here (and also §§5, 43–47), ownership of a slave, as in §§55, 76, 80, 84, 85, 86, and the status of being a manumitted slave, a freedman who would continue under the patronage of their manumitters, as in §3: see Crone, "Mawlā."

3 Many Arabic works from the classical period were dictated, and we often find indications of this. Even when books were written down by their author (as opposed to being dictated to an amanuensis), they often preserve this gesture of orality by continuing the practice of using indications of orality such as "he (i.e., the author) said." See §§2, 6, 7, 27, 28, 47, 48, 49, 50, 69, 71, 73, 74, 89, for the instances of this use of "he said" in the text.

4 The word rendered as "representative" is *safīr*, the modern Arabic for "ambassador." It seems that Nadhīr, a high-ranking member of the caliphal court, presented the letter from the king of the Volga Bulghārs to the caliph and so acted in an ambassadorial role, as the

king's representative or go-between. His *mawlā* (freedman, manumitted slave) Sawsan, in turn, represents Nadhīr on the embassy and is therefore called the "envoy" (*rasūl*). Ibn Faḍlān represents the caliph.

5 This "medication" is presented to the king in §41 ("unguents"). It later featured prominently as the reason for the king's conversion to Islam: see DeWeese, *Islamization*, 72–81, especially 76–78.

6 Ibn Faḍlān records some thirty days of stopover time at the fourteen halting posts at this stage of their journey.

7 Literally, "five days." Presumably, Ibn Faḍlān means that Aḥmad ibn Mūsā—who was to sell the estate of Arthakhushmīthan and provide the embassy with the money required by the Bulghār king to build the fort—left Baghdad on the fifth day (reckoning inclusively) after the party's departure, on the sixteenth of Safar (June 25).

8 The word translated as "soldier" is *ghulām*. It can denote any man, free or slave, closely bound in service to his master. I have rendered it variously as "soldier," "retainer," "man," and "male slave." See Sourdel, "Ghulām: 1," and Bosworth, "Ghulām: 2."

9 A curious echo of Q Nisā' 4:121: «Their destination is Jahannam. They will find no way to escape.»

10 See Q Insān 76:13. *Zamharīr* is explained as the burning cold of Hell.

11 From late November–early December, 921 to the end of February, 922.

12 This is a crucial instance of an awkward term in the text, *bayt*, which can designate variously a "tent," a "chamber," or a "house." Here the word *bayt* is contrasted with the other predominant term for "tent" in the text, *qubbah*, properly a "domed structure," rendered here and elsewhere as "yurt." I am unsure what, exactly, is descibed by the phrase "a chamber inside another chamber." The alternative is to render the phrase as "a tent inside another tent, with a Turkish yurt of animal skins inside it."

13 This is the only mention in the extant text of the involvement of Sawsan's "brother-in-law." The "jurists and instructors" mentioned in §3 are here reduced to one jurist and one instructor.

14 I take the point to be that the Turk does not recognize God as a member of the Turkic pantheon. According to Canard, *Voyage*, 102, n. 74, the caliph is intended by the word *rabb*.

15 It is possible that Ibn Faḍlān is drawing a more exact picture, so the phrase may mean that they used their clothes to fan the flames, causing sparks to leap from the fire. I thank Professor Philip Kennedy for this suggestion.

16 That is, on the morning of 17 Dhu l-Qaʿdah, 309 (Tuesday, March 19, 922).

17 I translate the phrase *idhā bi-* with this and similar expressions, of varying emphasis. I want to bring out the strong presence of eyewitness testimony, which predominates in Ibn Faḍlān's account.

18 An allusion to Q Muddaththir 74:50–51. See also §76.

19 This is a key instance in the text of an ambiguous use of the Arabic term *rabb* in Ibn Faḍlān's account of the Turks and the Rūsiyyah. As a form of address, *rabb* can be applied to a human in a position of leadership, but is often reserved for addressing God. The point Ibn Faḍlān makes about monotheism and reason is that the Ghuzziyyah Turks have neither revealed law nor a set of social customs based upon natural law determined through the use of reason. Ibn Faḍlān's picture of them reveals that they are henotheists who base their social practices on a strict code, though he apparently does not think this qualifies as *ʿaql*, reason.

20 Q Shūrā 42:38.

21 This is the first mention in the text of an interpreter.

22 The Mashhad MS reading *tagharrasa* is an unattested form. I suspect it conveys a notion that the bather has "planted" something in the water he washes in.

23 I thank Professor Geert Jan van Gelder for explaining this use of *qāma ʿalā* to me.

24 An echo of Q Yūsuf 12:23.

25 There is a lacuna of one word in the manuscript.

26 The term used is *al-jannah*, a standard Arabic term for Paradise. It recurs regularly throughout the treatise when reference is made to

the Turkic or Rūsiyyah otherworld. In Yāqūt §4.4, the structure in which the Khazar *khāqān* is buried is called "the Garden."

27 The Arabic expression rendered as "those who" is highly irregular: *-hum man* (pronominal suffix with *man* as relative), for the relative pronoun *alladhīna* or simply *man* without the suffix *-hum*.

28 In accordance with the custom described in §23.

29 But not his birth mother, in accordance with the custom described in §22.

30 This statement seems to imply that Ibn Faḍlān was not familiar with the practice of sheep shearing.

31 A paraphrase of Q Isrā' 17:43.

32 The last two rivers listed are normally identified as follows: the Jāwshīn is changed to Jāwshīz and is thought to be either the Aqtāy or the Gausherma, and the Bnāsnah is usually written as Niyāsnah. However, these rivers are located north of the region in which Ibn Faḍlān encounters the king of the Bulghārs. McKeithen observes that: "Ibn Faḍlān here takes the opportunity to account for all the rivers that were crossed by him during his stay in the land of the Ṣaqālibah" (*Risālah*, 82, n. 232). It is possible, of course, that completely different rivers may be intended and that Ibn Faḍlān may not be in a rush at this point in the text to list all the rivers he traversed irrespective of their geographical locations, so I have not altered the spelling of the river names.

33 Ibn Faḍlān is reckoning inclusively, counting the day the caravan departed, the second of Dhu l-Qaʿdah, and the day it arrived.

34 The medication referred to in §3.

35 Presumably the other kings get their share of the meal also.

36 The translation of this phrase is conjectural. It is usually explained in terms of fermentation—that is, letting it sit for a day and a night means the drink does not develop intoxicating properties and so would be permissible for Muslims to drink. If this is the meaning, then I would translate: "so called because it takes a day and a night to make." But Ibn Faḍlān's text does not say that he and the envoys drank the wine but that they rose to their feet three times while the king drank

and delivered his oath. It is Yāqūt's quotation of the passage that adds the verb *wa-sharibnā*, "and we drank."

37 This is one of two places in the text where the title "king of the Bulghārs" is used, rather than "king of the Ṣaqālibah": see also §69.

38 "God's bondsman" is the meaning of the name ʿAbdallāh. For the fuller version of the hadith, see *Risālat Ibn Faḍlān*, ed. al-Dahhān, 118 and n. 1.

39 As explained in §6.

40 Commentators and translators rarely agree that the king's remarks imply that Ibn Faḍlān was an Arab. Canard, *Voyage*, 109, n. 163, thinks that the term *ustādh*, "master," cannot refer to the caliph but only to the vizier. I suspect that the king intends Nadhīr al-Ḥaramī by the term.

41 This was in §14.

42 The *iqāmah* is a second call to stand in prayer, uttered after the *adhān* by the muezzin, as he stands behind the imam, when the latter is about to begin leading prayer. It consists of the text of the *adhān*, with the addition of the phrase *qad qāmat al-ṣalāt*, "prayer has begun." According to Shāfiʿī practice as observed by the caliphal court, the formulae taken from the *adhān* were uttered once in the *iqāmah*, and *qad qāmat al-ṣalāt* was uttered twice, whereas, according to Ḥanafī practice—the practice (*madhhab*) followed by the Samanids of Bukhara and to which the Bulghārs and the other steppe Turks converted—all the formulae were uttered twice. See the detailed note by Canard, *Voyage*, 110–11, n. 165. My thanks go to Professor Shawkat Toorawa for explaining this to me.

43 What the king means by this reference to the first caliph, renowned for his honesty, is unclear.

44 The *sāʿah qiyāsiyyah* refers to a practice of dividing night and day into twelve hours: "the clock worked on 'unequal' hours, that is, the hours of daylight or darkness were divided by twelve to give hours that varied in length from day to day" (Hill, "Sāʿa," 655). A proportional hour may thus be longer or shorter than an astronomical hour, depending on latitude and time of the year. I am grateful to Professor van Gelder for this explanation.

45 The Qur'an was divided into seven equal portions for recitation over the seven days of the week: see von Denffer, *'Ulūm al-Qur'ān*, 69–70. My thanks go to Professor Toorawa for the reference.

46 This is an indication that Ibn Faḍlān remained with the Bulghārs until the end of the summer and so presumably would not have made the crossing of the Ustyurt back to Khwārazm until the following spring, at the earliest. Markwart, "Ein arabischer Bericht über die arktischen (uralischen) Länder," 279–80 and 331–32, argues, in terms of astronomical data, that Ibn Faḍlān's claim (that this took place on the night of May 12–13) cannot be an accurate assessment of the hours of daylight in May. He prefers to see this as taking place in July. According to Czeglédy, "Zur Meschheder Handschrift," 225–27, Ibn Faḍlān is organizing his narrative by type of observation. See also McKeithen, *Risālah*, 97, n. 283. The "boiling cooking pot" is a trope of geographical lore concerning the northern regions in Arabic texts. The conversation with the muezzin revolves around the organization of the day in terms of the five ritual prayers: see Monnot, "Ṣalāt."

47 This is the only allusion to the return of the embassy I can detect in the account (aside from the fact of the preservation of the account itself).

48 The passage is obscure and can mean either that the Bulghār word for "female slaves" is the same as that for "apples" or that the apples are called something like "slave apples." Perhaps Ibn Faḍlān picked up a smattering of Bulghār or else acquired this information from the interpreter or a local informant.

49 The Prophet Muḥammad was also known as Aḥmad: see Q Ṣaff 61:6. Both names derive from the same triliteral root pattern in Arabic. The Bulghār's name is Ṭālūt, the Qur'anic name for Saul: Q Baqarah 2:247–49. McKeithen, *Risālah*, 111, n. 335, suggests that Ibn Faḍlān may be endeavoring to represent a Turkic name.

50 These are Q 1, Sūrat al-Fātiḥah and 112, Sūrat al-Ikhlāṣ, respectively.

51 The Arabic states: "there is not one of them whose bottom can be attained."

52 This is the market the Rūsiyyah use in §74.

53 It seems that Gog and Magog are separated from the outside world by both a gate and a wall.

54 It seems that the Wīsū are surprisingly knowledgeable about the Muslim apocalyptic legends of Gog and Magog. The reference to "the Wall" is to the wall that the Qur'an says the Horned Man (Alexander the Great) built to imprison Gog and Magog. For analogues in Arabic sources to the fabulous fish that feeds Gog and Magog, see Canard, *Voyage*, 116, n. 228. The *qāla* that occurs at this point in the text is the *qāla* that indicates that someone has finished speaking.

55 There is a lacuna of one word in the manuscript.

56 The text of the Mashhad manuscript is obscure. Lunde and Stone, *Ibn Fadlān*, 43, translate: "and if a woman from Khwārazm is present." I have adopted their rendering. They explain this in terms of the requirement that a corpse must be washed by a Muslim woman; as the nearest source of Muslim women was Khwārazm, they infer that "Islam had not extended to Bulghār females" (228, n. 79).

57 See §33, where the Ghuzziyyah are forced to pay the same tribute.

58 See Yāqūt §4.4, for how these hostage brides fare at the Khazar court.

59 This phrase is obscure and the Arabic syntax is far from clear. Ibn Faḍlān is thought by many to be describing tattoos of trees and other forms, but the practice of tattooing is unattested for the Vikings and he may mean that they have the images of trees and other shapes painted on them, perhaps using a plant dye.

60 Viking women often wore a scoop for ear-wax, together with other items for personal grooming, attached to a chain worn around the neck or under a broach. It is this scoop that Ibn Faḍlān calls a knife.

61 A second occurrence of this allusion to Q Muddaththir 74:50–51; see the account of the Ghuzziyyah at §18.

62 Ibn Faḍlān's Arabic implies that, for the Rūsiyyah, this communal wash is a binding ritual.

63 Ibn Faḍlān shows that he is aware that the funerary practice of the Rūsiyyah is not fixed but admits variation based upon wealth. See §71 for a similar recognition of variation in Bulghār funerary ritual based upon tribal status. Variations in the funerary practice of the

Ghuzziyyah seem to depend on tribal membership and wealth: see §27.

64 Professor van Gelder refers me to al-Tanūkhī's *Nishwār al-muḥādarah*, 2:184.1–185.4 for an anecdote that revolves around the term *jawānbīrah*, an arabicized borrowing from Persian which appears to mean a "middle-aged" woman. I suspect, though I have no hard evidence, that, with this unusual phrase, Ibn Faḍlān may be trying to communicate a more menacing aspect of the Angel of Death than simply telling us her age.

65 See §27 for the "Garden" of the Ghuzziyyah and Yāqūt §4.4 for the "Garden" of the *khāqān* of the Khazars.

66 See, e.g., §72 for the vassalage of the king of the Bulghārs.

67 Wüstenfeld 1.112.16–113.15 = §68.

68 Wüstenfeld 1.468.17–469.15 = §§37–38.

69 Yāqūt lists thirteen deities—fourteen, if we include the sky god.

70 An echo of Q Isrā' 17:43.

71 Wüstenfeld 1.723.19–727.21 = §§2–4, 39–44, 48–50, 51, 53–56, 59, 61–63.

72 The scribe writes "Asad," clearly an error for Rāshid.

73 Wüstenfeld 2.436.20–440.6 = §90. This passage is, in fact, a quotation from al-Iṣṭakhrī's *Kitāb Masālik*, 220.1–222.3. See Dunlop, *The History of the Jewish Khazars*, 89–115, especially 91–95 and 96–97. On this lemma, see my comments on pp. xxxiv–xxxv.

74 The name means "Black Khazars."

75 This is the point at which the Mashhad manuscript ends.

76 Klyashtorny, "About One Khazar Title," argues that this word is an abbreviation of a Turkic honorific that he explains as "head of the royal falcon hunting."

77 In view of the association in Ibn Faḍlān's text between tents, illnesses, death, and burial practices I have opted here to render *bayt* as "tent," though "chamber" may equally be intended. See above, n. 12.

78 The identity of 'they' is not specified in the text. Presumably the Khazars generally are meant, and not, as in the following sentence, the men who actually place the *khāqān* in his grave.

79 Noonan, “Some Observations,” 208, infers from this number that the Khazar *khāqān* ruled “over 25 distinct peoples.”

80 The year 310 H began on May 1, 922.

81 Wüstenfeld 2.484.10–485.23 = §§8–11.

82 ʿAbdallāh is Yāqūt.

83 See Q Insān 76:13.

84 Wüstenfeld 2.834.18–840.12 = §§74–89.

85 See Q Muddaththir 74:50–51.

86 This is how the word is written in the edition. It seems to be a hybrid of *khadhank* and *khalanj*.

Glossary of Names and Terms

ʿAbdallāh ibn Bāshtū al-Khazarī (§§3, 6, 8) the name of the Khazar who serves as the envoy from the king of the Bulghārs to the caliphal court. To judge by his name, ʿAbdallāh, he is a Muslim, a fact that has led some to suspect that he was a political activist working against the Khazar khaqanate.

The name of his father is transcribed as "Bāšto" by Togan (*Reisebericht*, 3), "Bachtū" by Canard (*Voyage*, 28: see 96, n. 10), and "Bāshtū" by McKeithen (*Risālah*, 27–28 and n. 14) and Lunde and Stone (*Ibn Fadlān*, 3). It is not clear whether the final *alif* has a phonetic value or is *alif al-wiqāyah*, to indicate that the *wāw* is a long final vowel ū.

See Golden, *Khazar Studies*, 1:160–62.

Abū Bakr (§47) Abū Bakr al-Ṣiddīq (r. 11–13/632–34), the first of the four rightly-guided caliphs, dubbed "the Veracious" (al-Ṣiddīq). The Bulghār king calls Ibn Faḍlān "Abū Bakr the Veracious." Just what the king means by this reference is not clear.

Adhl (§34) the fourth river crossed by the caravan, on portable, collapsible camel-skin rafts, after its departure from the territory of the Ghuzziyyah.

The name is transcribed as "Od̲ïl" by Togan (*Reisebericht*, 32, n. 6), who identifies it as the modern river Uyïl (or Oyïl), as does Kovalevskiĭ (*Kniga*, 191, n. 303). "Uzil/Uïl": Canard, *Voyage*, 48, 107, n. 134; "Udhil": McKeithen, *Risālah*, 76, n. 199; "Ūdhil/Uil": Lunde and Stone, *Ibn Fadlān*, 22, 226, n. 45; "Udil": Frye, *Ibn Fadlān's Journey*, 42. Frye (*Ibn Fadlān's Journey*, 97) gives its contemporary name as the "Oyil"; in Róna-Tas's map (*Hungarians and Europe*, 223) it is the Uil.

*Āfr*n* (§4) an otherwise unattested name of the Ṭāhirid outpost which the embassy reaches after crossing the Āmul desert. Popular candidates for the location are: Āfrīr (al-Dahhān, *Risālah*, 76, n. 1); Firabr (McKeithen, *Risālah*, 33–34, n. 42); Afirabr (Lunde and Stone, *Ibn Fadlān*, 4, 224, n. 18). It is probably a scribal error for Firabr, which seems the likeliest: Canard, *Voyage*, 97, n. 26.

Aḥmad ibn ʿAlī (§4) a member of the caliphal force sent to combat Yūsuf ibn Abī l-Sāj, the ruler of Azerbaijan who had, in 304/916, ousted Muḥammad ibn ʿAlī Ṣuʿlūk, the Samanid governor of Rayy, Aḥmad's own brother. After the defeat of Yūsuf ibn Abī l-Sāj, Aḥmad ibn ʿAlī was given control of Isfahan and Qum, and Rayy was put under the control of ʿAlī ibn Wahsudhān. On the assassination of ʿAlī ibn Wahsudhān, Ahmad ibn ʿAlī took control of Rayy without caliphal authority. Baghdad sent Muḥammad ibn Sulaymān, Ibn Faḍlān's patron, against him, but Muḥammad died in the campaign. Baghdad subsequently recognized Aḥmad ibn ʿAlī as the Abbasid governor of Rayy. He died in 311/924.

See Canard, *Voyage*, 96–97, n. 20; McKeithen, *Risālah*, 31, n. 28.

Aḥmad ibn Faḍlān ibn al-ʿAbbās ibn Rāshid ibn Ḥammād (§§1, 3, 14, 40–41, 44–47, 48–53, 58–59, 61, 63, 66–68, 70–71, 73–74, 80, 82, 88; Yāqūt §§1.1, 1.3, 2.1–2.2, 3.1–3.3, 3.6–3.7, 3.9–3.10, 4.1, 5.1, 5.4, 5.6, 5.11, 6.1, 6.9–6.10) the representative of the caliph al-Muqtadir on the embassy, delegated to read the official correspondence from Baghdad, to superintend the presentation of gifts to the Bulghār king and other local dignitaries, and to supervise the jurists and instructors sent with the embassy to instruct the Volga Bulghārs. Before the mission, he had been under the sponsorship of the powerful military commander Muḥammad ibn Sulaymān.

Aḥmad ibn Mūsā al-Khwārazmī (§5) an otherwise unknown person, whose role in the embassy was to take over the running of the estate in Arthakhushmīthan and, presumably, provide the envoys with the money required by the Bulghār king to build his fort.

Akhtī (§34) the seventh river crossed by the caravan, on portable, collapsible camel-skin rafts, after its departure from Ghuzziyyah territory.

Togan (*Reisebericht*, 33, n. 2), makes several suggestions as to which modern river it corresponds: the Buldurti, the Ashshi-Say, or the Ashshi-Ölenti. Kovalevskiĭ (*Kniga*, 192, n. 304) identifies it as the Ankaty. It is the "Ankhati/Grand Ankati" according to Canard (*Voyage*, 107, n. 134, though the name of the river is omitted in his translation), the "Akhatī" according to McKeithen (*Risālah*, 76, n. 202), and the "Akhtī/Ankati" according to Lunde and Stone (*Ibn Fadlān*, 22, 226, n. 45). Frye (*Ibn Fadlān's Journey*, 97) transcribes it as "Akhati" and identifies it as the modern "Ankaty or Buldurti," which corresponds to the Ankati on Róna-Tas's map (*Hungarians and Europe*, 223).

ʿAlī ibn Abī Ṭālib (§9; Yāqūt §5.4) cousin and son-in-law of the Prophet Muḥammad and the fourth, and last, of the rightly-guided caliphs (r. 35–40/656–61), greatly revered by Shiʿis. The cursing of ʿAlī referred to in the text may be a survival from the days of Umayyad rule.

Almish, Son of Shilkī see al-Ḥasan, Son of Yilṭawār.

Āmul (§4) not to be confused with Āmul, the capital of Ṭabaristān, this is a city on the river Jayḥūn (Oxus, modern Amu Darya), present-day Chardzhou or Turkmenabat. Āmul marks an important crossing-place of the Jayḥūn on the historic route from Nishapur and Marw to Transoxania and beyond. The town of Farab (or Farabr/Firabr), a dependency of Bukhara, lay on the opposite bank.

See Togan, *Reisebericht*, 6, n. 2; Kovalevskiĭ, *Kniga*, 168, n. 62; Le Strange, *Lands*, 403–4.

Ardkwā (§9) a place in Khwārazm otherwise unattested, the inhabitants of which are known as al-Kardaliyyah.

The commentators and translators, unable to decide on whether the *wāw* has a phonetic or simply a phonemic value, differ in transcribing the toponym: "Ardakuwâ," according to Canard (*Voyage*, 33, 100, n. 50); "Ardkwa," according to Frye (*Ibn Fadlān's Journey*, 30, who renders the name of the inhabitants as "Ardakiwa"); "Ardakū or Ardakūwa," according to Lunde and Stone (*Ibn Fadlān*, 8, 225, n. 28).

Ardn (§34) the fifth river crossed by the caravan, on portable, collapsible camel-skin rafts, after its departure from Ghuzziyyah territory.

Togan (*Reisebericht*, 32, n. 7) suggests it is the modern Zhaqsibay (now dried up), just north of the Aral Sea. It is the "Erden" according to Canard (*Voyage*, 48, 107, n. 134) who may take this form from Kovalevskiĭ (*Kniga*, 130), the "Ardan," according to McKeithen (*Risālah*, 76, n. 200), and even the "ʿArdin" (with a *ʿayn*), according to Lunde and Stone (*Ibn Fadlān*, 22, 226, n. 45). It is the modern "Zhaqsibay or Kaldigayti," according to Frye (*Ibn Fadlān's Journey*, 97); on Róna-Tas's map (*Hungarians and Europe*, 223), it is the Kaldyigayti.

Arthakhushmīthan (§§3, 5) one of the estates of Ibn al-Furāt in Khwārazm, according to Ibn Faḍlān.

Yāqut (*Muʿjam al-Buldān*, 1.191.11) vocalizes it as *arthakhushmīthan*. The Mashhad manuscript reads *arnkhshmthīn* at folio 197a.7 and *artkhshmthīn* at folio 197b.8. Kovalevskiĭ (*Kniga*, 122) suggests Arsakhushmisan, and Krachkovskiĭ (*Puteshestvie*, 56) reads Artakhushmathin, but neither elaborates on their readings. Barthold (*Turkestan*, 148) suggests that it corresponds to modern Khojayli, in the Karakalpakstan region of Uzbekistan. Canard (*Voyage*, 96, n. 9) and McKeithen (*Risālah*, 27, n. 11) provide references to this location in other Arabic sources.

Askil (§§69, 72) the name of a clan subject to the Bulghār king, given as Asghl by Ibn Rustah (*Kitāb al-Aʿlāq*, 141.11). Their king is allied to the Bulghār king through marriage. The clan seems to seek to dissociate itself from the Bulghār king's conversion to Islam.

The tribal name is generally translated as a personal name: e.g., "King Eskel" by Frye (*Ibn Fadlān's Journey*, 59). See Zimonyi, *Origins*, 48–49; Golden, *Introduction*, 254; Róna-Tas, *Hungarians and Europe*, 225.

Atrak, Son of al-Qaṭaghān (§§30–33) the military commander (*sü-baši*) of the Ghuzziyyah Turks, who receives a letter from Nadhīr al-Ḥaramī, the embassy's representative in Baghdad.

There is some discussion as to whether the name of his father, written as *al-qṭʿān* in the manuscript, is a title or a proper name: Togan (*Reisebericht*, 142) discerns a Mongol origin. The Mashhad scribe writes the word with *ʿayn* where others see a *ghayn*: thus Togan

(*Reisebericht*, 142); Kovalevskiĭ (*Kniga*, 188); Canard (*Voyage*, 105, n. 114); al-Dahhān (*Risālah*, 101); McKeithen (*Risālah*, 69, n. 175).

See Golden, *Introduction*, 209; Róna-Tas, *Hungarians and Europe*, 225 for the use of *ghayn* and *kāf* in Arabic transcriptions of Turkic words after the sixth/twelfth century.

Azkhn (§36) the third river crossed by the caravan, on portable, collapsible camel-skin rafts, after its departure from Bajanāk territory.

It is "Irkhiz (Irgiz)" according to Kovalevskiĭ (*Kniga*, 192), Canard (*Voyage*, 49: see 107, n. 138), and McKeithen (*Risālah*, 78, n. 212). It is "Arkhaz/Irgiz" accoding to Lunde and Stone (*Ibn Fadlān*, 23, 226, n. 46); "Azhin" according to Frye (*Ibn Fadlān's Journey*, 42), who identifies it as the modern "Irgiaz or Talovka" (*Ibn Fadlān's Journey*, 97). According to Togan, who reads *azḥn* (*Reisebericht*, 34, n. 3), it may refer to a small river between Chaghan and Mocha. On Róna-Tas's map (*Hungarians and Europe*, 223), it is the Irgiz.

Bājā' (§36) the fourth river crossed by the caravan, on portable, collapsible camel-skin rafts, after its departure from Bajanāk territory.

This a further instance of the Mashhad scribe using a *'ayn* where modern scholars would see a *ghayn*: *bājāgh*. Togan (*Reisebericht*, 34, n. 4) suggests it is the modern river Mocha. Kovalevskiĭ (*Kniga*, 192) follows Togan. It is "Bâtchâgh/Motchka," according to Canard (*Voyage*, 49: see 107, n. 138); and "Bājāgh," according to al-Dahhān (*Risālah*, 107, n. 4); McKeithen (*Risālah*, 78, n. 213); Lunde and Stone (*Ibn Fadlān*, 23, 226, n. 46). Frye (*Ibn Fadlān's Journey*, 97) identifies the "Bajagh" as the modern "Mocha"; on Róna-Tas's map (*Hungarians and Europe*, 223), it is the Mocha.

Bajanāk (§§35–36) Petchenegs, a nomadic or semi-nomadic Turkic people first reported east of the Caspian Sea and the second Turkic tribe encountered by the embassy on its route to the Volga Bulghārs. During the third/ninth century, they migrated west, under pressure from the Ghuzziyyah. The Petchenegs, allies of the Byzantines, constituted an important force on the Pontic steppes and further west, near Kievan Rus. By the late third/ninth century they had driven the Magyars to the Pannonian lowlands, where the state of Hungary was established.

bāk (Yāqūt §4.2) one of the titles of the vice-regent, that is, the non-khaganal ruler of the Khazars.

See Golden, *Khazar Studies*, 1:184–85; Golden, *Introduction*, 240; Róna-Tas, *Hungarians and Europe*, 233.

bakand (§§11, 26; Yāqūt §5.10) according to Ibn Faḍlān, he heard this Khwārazmian word for "bread" in Khwārazm and among the Ghuzziyyah.

Baranjār, al- (§66) the name of a clan whose conversion to Islam was supervised by Ibn Faḍlān. The name has been associated with the Khazar settlement in the Caucasus known as Balanjār.

See McKeithen, *Risālah*, 111, n. 334; Golden, *Khazar Studies*, 1:221–24 ("Bālānjār"); Zimonyi, *Origins*, 49 ("Baranjār/Balanjar"); Frye, *Ibn Fadlān's Journey*, 99; Róna-Tas, *Hungarians and Europe*, 224.

Bārs al-Ṣaqlābī (§§3, 13, 52) one of the *ghulāms*, presumably a slave-soldier who accompanied the embassy. In the context of the account, his affiliation, indicated by the name al-Ṣaqlābī, would not necessarily identify him as a Bulghār but possibly as a member of the subject population of the Bulghār king. It is uncertain whether he is the Bārs who led a rebellion of four thousand Turk cavalry in an attack on Baghdad in 296/908: McKeithen, *Risālah*, 28, n. 17. The name is usually transcribed as "Bāris," and scholars disagree whether the origin of the name Bārs is Slavic (= Boris) or Turkic (meaning "leopard"): Canard, *Voyage*, 28, 96, n. 11; Lunde and Stone, *Ibn Fadlān*, 4, 223, n. 11.

Bāshghird (§§37–38; Yāqūt §2.1–2.2.) Bashkirs, the last tribe encountered before the embassy arrives at the confluence of the Volga and Kama. Not much is known about the Bashkirs in the fourth/tenth century, although they are mentioned in several Arabic-language geographical treatises as occupying territory in the Ural mountains.

Baykand (§5) a town between Āmul and Bukhara, some two *farsakh*s from the latter.

See Le Strange, *Lands*, 463; Barthold, *Turkestan*, 117–19; Kovalevskiĭ, *Kniga*, 168, n. 65.

Bāynāj (§38) the fourth river crossed by the caravan after its departure from Bāshghird territory.

The Mashhad scribe writes it as "yā*nāj" with an undotted consonant. It should be read "Bāynākh," according to Togan (*Reisebericht*, 37, n. 4), and Kovalevskiĭ (*Kniga*, 194, n. 342) thinks it is the modern river Mayna. It is "Bâinakh," according to Canard (*Voyage*, 51: see also 108, n. 145). It is "Bāynākh," according to al-Dahhān (*Risālah*, 110, n. 4), McKeithen (*Risālah*, 81, n. 229), and Lunde and Stone (*Ibn Fadlān*, 24, 226, n. 49). Frye (*Ibn Fadlān's Journey*, 97) gives it as the modern "Mania" (a misspelling of Maina/Mayna); on Róna-Tas's map (*Hungarians and Europe*, 223), it is the Mayna.

Bghndī (§34) the first river crossed by the caravan, on portable, collapsible camel-skin rafts, after its departure from Ghuzziyyah territory.

The name is transcribed variously, with an initial *yā'* or *bā'*: "Yaghandî/Tchagan" by Canard (*Voyage*, 48, 106, n. 128); McKeithen (*Risālah*, 73, n. 192); "Yaghindī" by al-Dahhān (*Risālah*, 104, n. 5); so too Frye (*Ibn Fadlān's Journey*, 41) and Lunde and Stone (*Ibn Fadlān*, 22, 226, n. 45). Togan (*Reisebericht*, 32, n. 3) suggests it may be the modern Zhayïndï, near the river Emba. Kovalevskiĭ (*Kniga*, 191) believes it to be the river Chagan near Uralsk (Oral), in northwest Kazakhstan; on Róna-Tas's map (*Hungarians and Europe*, 223), it may be the Chagan. Frye (*Ibn Fadlān's Journey*, 97) identifies it as the "Zhayindi."

Bīr tankrī (§18) a Turkic phrase translated and explained by Ibn Faḍlān as meaning "By God, by the One." Tengri was the Turkic sky-god.

See Canard, *Voyage*, 38, 103, n. 83; McKeithen, *Risālah*, 54–55, ns. 129–30.

Bnāsnh (§38) the sixth river crossed by the caravan after its departure from Bāshghird territory.

Togan (*Reisebericht*, 37 and 38, n. 6) has "Nbāsnh" but suggests that it is to be read as "Nyāsnah," after Marquart, as does Kovalevskiĭ (*Kniga*, 194). It is "Niyasnah," according to Canard (*Voyage*, 51: see 108, n. 145), "Niyāsanah," according to McKeithen (*Risālah*, 82, n. 231), and "Nīyāsnah," according to Lunde and Stone, who do not venture a modern identification (*Ibn Fadlān*, 25, 226, n. 49). It does not appear on Róna-Tas's map (*Hungarians and Europe*, 223).

Bukhara (§§5–8; Yāqūt §§5.1–5.2) capital of the Samanid dynasty.

See Le Strange, *Lands*, 460–63; Barthold, *Turkestan*, 100–17; Barthold [Frye], "Bukhārā."

Bulghār/Bulghārs (§§39–73; Yāqūt §§1.1, 1.3, 3.1–3.10, 4.2, 4.3) the destination of the embassy. The Turkic Volga Bulghārs established their state at the confluence of the Volga and Kama rivers during the third/ninth century. By the beginning of the fourth/tenth century they had entered into a dynamic trading relationship with the Samanids in Central Asia, whereby their territory became one of the principal emporia of the period, rivaling and, ultimately, outlasting those of the Khazars. The Volga Bulghārs adopted Islam in the early fourth/tenth century and remained Muslims until the demise of their state in the wake of the attacks of the Mongols and their subsequent integration into the Golden Horde.

City of Peace (§§4, 5, 13; Yāqūt §3.2) the name used in the text for Baghdad, properly speaking the original Round City of Baghdad, founded by the caliph al-Manṣūr.

Commander of the Faithful (§§2, 5, 8, 9, 40, 43–47, 69, 73; Yāqūt §§2.1, 3.2, 3.5) a rendering of *amīr al-mu'minīn*, a title held by the caliphs.

dāʿī (§4) a reference in our text to the Zaydī al-Ḥāsan ibn al-Qāsim (d. 316/928). The title is used among several Muslim groups for their principal propagandists and missionaries. It became especially important in Shiʿi movements, where it was used as the title of the authorized spokesman of the spiritual leader, the Imam.

Al-Ḥāsan ibn al-Qāsim was known as al-Dāʿī li-l-Ḥaqq, "the Proselytizer for the Truth," and al-Dāʿī al-Ṣaghīr, "the Lesser Proselytizer," to distinguish him from al-Ḥasan ibn Zayd ibn Muḥammad (d. 270/884), al-Dāʿī al-Kabīr, "the Greater Proselytizer." His predecessor as ruler was his father-in-law, the warlord al-Ḥasan ibn ʿAlī al-Uṭrūsh (i.e., "the Deaf,"; d. 304/917). In 301/914 al-Uṭrūsh had wrested control of Ṭabaristān from the Samanids and captured its capital Āmul, thanks to an alliance with the local potentate Ibn Qārin mentioned in the text.

See Canard, *Voyage*, 97, n. 21; McKeithen, *Risālah*, 31, n. 32; Strothmann, "al-Ḥasan al-Uṭrūsh."

Dāmghān, al- (§4) the capital of the province of Qumis, on Ibn Faḍlān's route between Simnān and Nishapur; at the time of the mission it was under Zaydī control.

See Le Strange, *Lands*, 364–65.

dānaq (Yāqūt §5.4) a weight measure, one sixth of the *dīnār mithqāl*, the dinar used as a unit of weight; also here one-sixth of a dirham.

See Togan, *Reisebericht*, 112; Hinz, *Islamische Masse*, 11 (Persian, *dāng*).

Dār al-Bābūnj (Yāqūt §4.5) the unidentified location of a synagogue.

Togan (*Reisebericht*, 102–3, n. 4) speculates that it may have to do with the name Alphons or Adalphuns, thus "the house/dwelling of Alphons or Adalphuns." Kovalevskiĭ (*Kniga*, 273, n. 959) suggests it may be a woman's name.

See McKeithen, *Risālah*, 159, n. 559.

Daskarah, al- (§4) a town on Ibn Faḍlān's route between Nahrawān and Ḥulwān. It probably originated as a caravan post that, at the time of the mission, had developed into an important town on the Khurasan road.

See Le Strange, *Lands*, 62; Duri, "Daskarah."

dinar (§§14, 31, 45, 77; Yāqūt §§5.9, 6.4) an Islamic gold coin.

See Miles, "Dīnār."

dirham (§§7, 9, 11, 23, 39, 41, 45, 75, 77; Yāqūt §§3.4, 5.4, 5.8, 6.2, 6.4) a silver coin weighing usually about three grams and produced in enormous numbers. They circulated within the Islamic caliphate and were exported as payment for goods in long-distance trade. About half a million whole or fragmentary dirhams have been found across the vast trading networks of eastern and northern Europe. It is estimated that, during the first half of the fourth/tenth century alone, about 120 million dirhams were transported along the route taken by Ibn Faḍlān from the territory of the Samanids to the Volga Bulghārs.

See Miles, "Dirham."

Faḍl ibn Mūsā al-Naṣrānī, al- (§§5–6) an otherwise unknown person. The account notes that he was the fiscal agent of the estate in Arthakhushmīthan owned by the ousted vizier Ibn al-Furāt, which was to provide the envoys with the money required by the king of the Bulghārs to build his fort.

Falūs (§14) the name of the guide hired by the embassy in al-Jurjāniyyah and possibly representing *qılavuz*, a Turkic word for guide. Canard (*Voyage*, 102, n. 71) thinks it may be a "proto-Bulgharian honorific."

See Togan, *Reisebericht*, 17, n. 5; Lunde and Stone, *Ibn Faḍlān*, 225, n. 34.

farsakh (§§8, 39, 50, 53, 67; Yāqūt §§3.4, 3.7–3.8, 4.2-4.3, 5.2) a measure of distance, usually just short of six kilometers.

See Hinz, "Farsakh"; Hinz, *Islamische Masse*, 62 (Persian *farsaḫ*).

Gate of the Turks (§§5, 15) the name of a garrison outpost maintained at Zamjān by the Samanid emirate, on the edge of Turkic territories.

See Canard, *Voyage*, 102, ns. 72–73.

ghiṭrīfī dirham (§7) a low-value dirham that became the common currency in the region from the third/ninth century on. In theory, six *ghiṭrīfī* dirhams equaled one silver dirham, but there was considerable fluctuation in value. It was named after al-Ghiṭrīf ibn ʿAṭāʾ al-Jurashī who from 175 to 177 (ca. AD 791–93) was governor of Khurasan. According to legend, his brother al-Musayyab also minted coins known as *musayyabī* dirhams, but they were, in fact, named after an earlier governor of Khurasan, al-Musayyab ibn Zuhayr al-Ḍabbī: see §14, 31. The *ghiṭrīfī* dirham became the common currency in the region from the third/ninth century onwards.

See Togan, *Reisebericht*, 111–13; Kovalevskiĭ, *Kniga*, 171, n. 85; Barthold, *Turkestan*, 204–7; Frye, *Notes on the Early Coinage*, 29–31; Bosworth, "al-Ghiṭrīf b. ʿAṭāʾ"; Frye, *Ibn Fadlān's Journey*, 88–90.

Ghuzziyyah (§§18–34) the Oghuz, also known in Arabic as the Ghuzz, the first Turkic tribe encountered by the embassy after crossing the Ustyurt. They were an important tribe, whose earliest recorded home was northeast of the Caspian Sea. In the fourth/tenth century they began moving west into the Khazar khaqanate and ultimately played a role in its downfall.

Gog and Magog (§68; Yāqūt §1.2) a ferocious people, trapped, according to the Qurʾan, by Dhū l-Qarnayn (Alexander the Great) behind a great wall (Q 18, Sūrat al-Kahf). The collapse of the wall signaled the onset of the End Time, when Gog and Magog would wreak destruction on the earth.

Hamadhān (§4) modern Hamadhan in Iran, a major town, the capital of the province known as the Jibāl, on Ibn Faḍlān's route between Qirmīsīn and Sāwah.

See Le Strange, *Lands*, 194–96, 227–29; Frye, "Hama<u>dh</u>ān."

Ḥāmid ibn al-ʿAbbās (§41; Yāqūt §3.4) a financier (223–311/837–923) who became especially prominent as vizier (306–11/918–23) during the reign of al-Muqtadir. He became al-Muqtadir's vizier in Jumada 306/November 918 and was in post at the time of the embassy. In Rabiʿ al-Thani 311/August 923 he was replaced by Ibn al-Furāt.

See Massignon, "Ḥāmid b. al-ʿAbbās"; van Berkel, *Accountants and Men of Letters*, 161–63.

Ḥammawayh Kūsā (§4) Ḥammawayh ibn ʿAlī, Samanid general and military commander of Khurasan. "Kūsā" is a nickname meaning "beardless." His formal title, *ṣāḥib jaysh Khurāsān* (field marshal of Khurasan), was the Arabic equivalent of the Persian title *sipahsālār*.

See Barthold, *Turkestan*, 240–41; Togan, *Reisebericht*, 5–6, n. 8; Canard, *Voyage*, 97, n. 22; McKeithen, *Risālah*, 32, n. 35.

Ḥasan, Son of Yilṭawār, al- (§2; Yāqūt §3.2) the name of the Bulghār king of the Ṣaqālibah, in the context of his letter to al-Muqtadir's court. Almish, son of Shilkī, is the name by which Atrak, son of al-Qaṭaghān, refers to him in a Turkic context in §33, when the Ghuzziyyah leaders are debating the fate of the embassy. Atrak also refers to the king as his "son-in-law." The quotation of §2, given by Yāqūt (§3.2), refers to the king in a third variant: Almis, son of Shilkī Bilṭawār (*blṭwār* is either a misreading of Yilṭawār by the scribe of the Mashhad manuscript or an Arabic attempt to represent a Bulghār pronunciation of the Turkic title *elteber*). The king acquires a fourth name in our text, Jaʿfar, son of ʿAbdallāh, and two new titles, "king of the Bulghārs" and "emir of the Bulghārs" (§44; Yāqūt §3.5). This is when Ibn Faḍlān sanctions the king's conversion to Islam by approving his Muslim name and gubernatorial title for the Friday oration. Ibn Rustah, *Kitāb al-Aʿlāq*, 141.9 refers to him as *almsh* and identifies him as a Muslim.

Most editors and translators of this passage (§2) provide a hybrid combination of the version of the name given in §33 and the version given by Yāqūt: so, for instance, Frye (*Ibn Fadlān's Journey*, 25) renders it as "Almish ibn Shilki the Yiltawar (Elteber)." See the explanation given for the reconstruction of the name by Lunde and Stone (*Ibn Fadlān*, 222, n. 3).

I can see no reason that the king should not be known by a variety of names in various regnal or tribal contexts. The version of his name given in §2, al-Ḥasan, son of the Elteber, declares his Muslim identity and expresses that he, unlike his father, is not a Khazar subordinate. It also aligns Ibn Faḍlān's information from 309/921 with the information provided about a decade earlier by Ibn Rustah about the Bulghār king's adoption of Islam. The version of his name given in §33 is entirely in keeping with the Turkic context in which it is used—it is used by a Ghuzziyyah chief who has not yet, as Ibn Faḍlān tells us, embraced Islam. The name the king acquires in §47 (Yāqūt §3.5) is emblematic of his integration into the Abbasid polity as the loyal subject of his patron al-Muqtadir.

See Zimonyi, *Origins*, 125–29; Róna-Tas, *Hungarians and Europe*, 225–26.

Ḥulwān (§4) a town on Ibn Faḍlān's route between al-Daskarah and Qirmīsīn.

See Le Strange, *Lands*, 191–92; Lockhart, "Ḥulwān."

Ibn Faḍlān see Aḥmad ibn Faḍlān.

Ibn al-Furāt (§§3, 5, 6) Abū l-Ḥasan ʿAlī ibn Muḥammad ibn Mūsā ibn al-Furāt (241–312/855–924), an important financier and politician in the early fourth/tenth century who had been deprived of the office of vizier at the time of the embassy and imprisoned. This is the reason that one of his mulcted estates could be used to provide the funding designated for building the Bulghār fort. He held the vizierate three times: from Rabiʿ al-Awwal 296/December 908 to Dhu l-Hijjah 299/July 912, from Dhu l-Hijjah 304/June 917 to Jumada 306/November 918, and from Rabiʿ al-Thani 311/August 923 to Rabiʿ al-Awwal 312/June 924.

Ibn Qārin (§4) Sharwīn ibn Rustam ibn Qārin, the *ispahbad* (local governor) of Firrīm, encountered by the embassy in al-Dāmghān; a descendant of the Qarinid dynasty of Ṭabaristān and ally of the Zaydī ruler al-Ḥasan ibn ʿAlī al-Uṭrūsh, in territories around the Caspian. He would have been no friend of the mission.

See Rekaya, "Ḳārinids"; Togan, *Reisebericht*, 5–6, n. 8; Canard, *Voyage*, 97, n. 21; Madelung, "The Minor Dynasties," 205.

Itil (§§50, 67, 68, 74; Yāqūt §§1.1–1.3, 4.2, 6.2, 6.3) the usual Arabic name for the river Volga and for the capital city of the Khazars on the banks of the Volga delta. It is used in the text also for the Bulghār trading emporium on the bank of the Volga.

See Golden, *Khazar Studies*, 1:224–29.

Jaʿfar (§44; Yāqūt §3.5) the given name of the caliph al-Muqtadir (Abū l-Faḍl Jaʿfar ibn Aḥmad al-Muʿtaḍid), conferred on the king of the Volga Bulghārs by Ibn Faḍlān to mark his membership in the Islamic polity.

Jākhā (§36) the second river crossed by the caravan, on portable, collapsible camel-skin rafts, after its departure from Bajanāk territory.

Togan (*Reisebericht*, 34, n. 2) and Kovalevskiĭ (*Kniga*, 192, n. 313) identify it as the river Chagan, a tributary of the Ural. It is "Jakhâ/Tchagan," according to Canard (*Voyage*, 49: and see 107, n. 138), and "Jākhā," according to McKeithen (*Risālah*, 78, n. 211) and Lunde and Stone (*Ibn Fadlān*, 23, 226, n. 46). Frye (*Ibn Fadlān's Journey*, 97) identifies it as the modern "Chagan"; on Róna-Tas's map (*Hungarians and Europe*, 223) it may be the Chagan. However, Togan and Kovalevskiĭ, followed by Canard, also identify the Bghndī as the Chagan. Perhaps the mission crossed the same river or tributaries of the same river twice.

Jākhsh (§34) the third river crossed by the caravan, on portable, collapsible camel-skin rafts, after its departure from Ghuzziyyah territory.

Togan (*Reisebericht*, 32, n. 5) and Kovalevskiĭ (*Kniga*, 191, n. 303) identify it as the Sağïz in Kazakhstan. It is "Jakhch/Saghiz," according to Canard (*Voyage*, 48, 107, n. 134); and "Jākhsh," according to McKeithen (*Risālah*, 76, n. 198) and Lunde and Stone (*Ibn Fadlān*, 22, 226, n. 45). Frye (*Ibn Fadlān's Journey*, 97) identifies it as the "Saghir"; on Róna-Tas's map (*Hungarians and Europe*, 223), it is the Sagiz.

Jām (§34) The second river crossed by the caravan, on portable, collapsible camel-skin rafts, after its departure from Ghuzziyyah territory.

Togan (*Reisebericht*, 32, n. 4) and Kovalevskiĭ (*Kniga*, 191, n. 302) identify it as the Emba. It is "Jam," according to Canard (*Voyage*, 48, 107, n. 134) or "Jām," according to McKeithen (*Risālah*, 76, n. 197) and Lunde and Stone (*Ibn Fadlān*, 22, 226, n. 45). Frye (*Ibn Fadlān's Journey*, 97) identifies it as the modern "Emba"; on Róna-Tas's map (*Hungarians and Europe*, 223), it is the Emba.

Jāwashīghar (Yāqūt §4.4) the title given to the deputy of the *kundur khāqān* among the Khazar. According to Klyashtorny the word is an abbreviation of an honorific that he explains as "head of the royal falcon hunting."

Transcribed as "Ǧāwšiġr" and "Ǧawšïġïr" by Togan (*Reisebericht*, 99 and 260–63), "Jâwchîghr" by Canard (*Voyage*, 85, 127, n. 343), "Jāwshīghr" by McKeithen (*Risālah*, 154–55, n. 546), "Jaushighir" by Frye (*Ibn Fadlān's Journey*, 75), and "Jawshīghīr" by Lunde and Stone (*Ibn Fadlān*, 55, 229, n. 88).

See Golden, *Khazar Studies*, 1:191–92; Klyashtorny, "About One Khazar Title."

Jāwshīn (§38) the seventh river crossed by the caravan, after its departure from Bāshghird territory.

Togan (*Reisebericht*, 38, n. 1) suggests that it may be the Aqtay. Kovalevskiĭ (*Kniga*, 194, n. 345) notes that it may also be read "Jawshīz." It is "Djawchîz," according to Canard (*Voyage*, 51: see also 108, n. 145), "Jāwshīz," according to al-Dahhān (*Risālah*, 110, n. 6) and McKeithen (*Risālah*, 82, n. 232), "Jaushir (or Jaushiz)," according to Frye (*Ibn Fadlān's Journey*, 43), and "Jāwshīr/Aqtay or Gausherma," according to Lunde and Stone (*Ibn Fadlān*, 25, 226, n. 49). Frye (*Ibn Fadlān's Journey*, 97) gives it as "Jawshir" and identifies it as the "Aqtay or Gausherma." Most scholars locate this river in Bulghār territory and note that Ibn Faḍlān here purports to have crossed a river before he could have reached it.

Jāwshīr (§69) a river in Bulghār territory, presumed to be the river referred to earlier in the Mashhad manuscript as Jāwshīn.

It is transcribed as "Jawchîz" by Canard (*Voyage*, 116, n. 237), as "Jāwshīz" by McKeithen (*Risālah*, 117–18, n. 367), and as "Jāwshīr/Aqtay" by Lunde and Stone (*Ibn Fadlān*, 42, 228, n. 75).

Jayhānī, al- (§5) several viziers of Bukhara had this affiliation. Ibn Faḍlān may be referring to the Jayhānī credited with a famous geographical work entitled *The Book of the Routes and the Realms* (*Kitāb al-Masālik wa-l-mamālik*), which has not survived.

See Pellat, "Al-Djayhānī"; Göckenjan and Zimonyi, *Orientalische Berichte*.

Jayḥūn (§§4, 10, 13; Yāqūt §5.4) the Oxus, an important river in Turkestan, known today as the Amu Darya.

See Spuler, "Āmū Darya."

Jaykh (§36) the first river crossed by the caravan, on portable, collapsible camel-skin rafts, after its departure from Bajanāk territory.

The word is written as *ḥ*j* by the Mashhad scribe. Togan (*Reisebericht*, 34, ns. 1 and 2) and Kovalevskiĭ (*Kniga*, 192, n. 311) identify it as the modern Ural. It is "Jaikh," according to Canard (*Voyage*, 49, 107, n. 137), "Jaykh," according to al-Dahhān (*Risālah*, 107, n. 1, and McKeithen, *Risālah*, 76, n. 210), and even "Jāyikh," according to Lunde and Stone (*Ibn Fadlān*, 23, 226, n. 46). Frye (*Ibn Fadlān's Journey*, 97) identifies it as the modern "Ural," which, in several local languages and dialects, was called "Jaykh," and in Kazakh-Kyrgyz, Zhayiq and in Bashkir, Yayiq (see Togan, *Reisebericht*, 34, n. 1); on Róna-Tas's map (*Hungarians and Europe*, 223) it is the Ural.

Jīt (§15) a way station known to some Arabic geographers, after the entry into the Ustyurt, via the Gate of the Turks, at Zamjān.

See Canard, *Voyage*, 102, ns. 72–73; McKeithen, *Risālah*, 51, ns. 116–17.

Jrmsān (§38) the first river crossed by the caravan after its departure from Bāshghird territory.

Togan (*Reisebericht*, 37, n. 1) and Kovalevskiĭ (*Kniga*, 194, n. 339) identify it as the Cheremshan (or Chirimshan), in Tatarstan. It is "Djaramsan," according to Canard (*Voyage*, 51), "Jaramshān," according to McKeithen (*Risālah*, 81, n. 226), and "Jirimshān" according to al-Dahhān (*Risālah*, 110, n. 1) and Lunde and Stone (*Ibn Fadlān*, 24, 226, n. 49). Frye (*Ibn Fadlān's Journey*, 97) identifies it as the "Chirimshan"; on Róna-Tas's map (*Hungarians and Europe*, 223) it is the Cheremshan.

Jurjāniyyah, al- (§§8, 10, 12, 14, 15, 23, 39; Yāqūt §§3.4, 5.2) Gurganj, Khwārazm's second city (commercially more vibrant than Kāth), probably corresponding, to some extent, to modern Konya-Urgench. Canard (*Voyage*, 99, n. 47) thinks that the distance of fifty *farsakh*s given by Ibn Faḍlān may be an exaggeration or a miscalculation.

See Le Strange, *Lands*, 445; Spuler, "Gurgandj."

Kardaliyyah, al- see Ardkwā.

Khadhank (§§34, 60, 69, 82, 88; Yāqūt §6.8) a type of tree thought by many to be the birch.

Róna-Tas (*Hungarians and Europe*, 226) argues that it is an Arabicized form of the Bulghār word for "birch," *hazing*.

See Canard, *Voyage*, 106–7, n. 131, 115, n. 210, 117, n. 243.

Khalanj (Yāqūt §6.7) a type of tree thought by some to be the maple, by others the birch, often confused with *khadhank*.

See Canard, *Voyage*, 106–7, n. 131.

khāqān (§90; Yāqūt §4.4) in Ibn Faḍlān's account, the title of the ruler of the Khazars. It is a well-known Turkic title of obscure origin. Among the Khazars the *khāqān* became increasingly sacral and taboo. The office had ceremonial aspects, and the *khāqān* could even be sacrificed in difficult times, according to al-Masʿūdī (*Murūj al-dhahab*, 1.215.3–7; and see §453, 1.214.14–215.9 generally).

See Golden, *Khazar Studies*, 1:192–96; Golden, "The Question of the Rus' Qağanate"; Golden, *Introduction*, 240.

Khāqān Bih (§90; Yāqūt §4.4) the title of the deputy of the Khazar *khāqān*. *Bih* is clearly cognate with *beg*, the old Turkic title for a tribal chieftain.

Canard (*Voyage*, 84, 126–27, n. 340) renders it "Khâqân Beg," McKeithen (*Risālah*, 154, n. 543) "Khāqān Beh," Frye (*Ibn Fadlān's Journey*, 75) "Khaqan Bih," and Lunde and Stone (*Ibn Fadlān*, 55) "khāqān beg."

See Golden, *Khazar Studies*, 1:162–65; Golden, *Introduction*, 240.

Khaz (Yāqūt §4.5) the title given to the Muslim *ghulām* of the Khazar *khāqān*, who had executive and judicial authority over the Muslims resident in the Khazar capital. Frye (*Ibn Fadlān's Journey*, 77) suggests "Khaz (Khan?)."

See Canard, *Voyage*, 87; McKeithen, *Risālah*, 159, n. 556; Lunde and Stone, *Ibn Fadlān*, 57, 229, n. 90.

Khazar/Khazars (§§1, 33, 67, 72; Yāqūt §§4.1–4.5) the most powerful Turkic group on the Eurasian steppe at the time of the mission, ruled by the *khāqān*. The Khazar khaqanate emerged in the early first/seventh century and remained for centuries the most important political entity on the Eurasian steppe. It occasionally entered into alliances with Byzantium and fought off Muslim incursions via the Caucasus in the first/seventh and second/eighth centuries, after which it established a more peaceful relationship with the caliphate, mainly through trade. The Arabic sources note that the Khazars converted at some point to Judaism, or at least the elite surrounding the khaqanal house did.

The description of the Khazar polity and regnal customs that exists only in the form of a quotation by Yāqūt seems to have been appended by Ibn Faḍlān (or, according to some, by a later redactor) as an addendum to his notice on the King of the Rūs. The embassy did not visit the Khazar khaqanate.

Khljh (§§67, 69) the name in the text for the three lakes where the embassy first meets the Bulghār king.

The lakes are identified by Kovalevskiĭ (*Kniga*, 218, n. 564) as the modern "Chistoe Ozero," "Kuryshevskoe Ozero," and "Atmanskoe Ozero." He believes that the word is akin to Chuvash *khel(-le)*, meaning "winter." According to Togan (*Reisebericht*, 38–39, n. 1, and 68) it is "Ḫalǧah," and he identifies it as the lakes of the village of Tri Ozera (Russian, "three lakes") some five or six kilometers from the Volga, just south of Bulghār, named Poganoe, Lebiad, and Troshchanoye. Canard (*Voyage*, 66) transcribes it as "Khallaja/Khelletché" and McKeithen (*Risālah*, 112, n. 339) as "Khallajah."

Khurasan (§§4–6, 47) a historical region of Persia and Turkestan. In Ibn Faḍlān's time its borders were marked approximately in the west by the towns of al-Dāmghān and Jurjān and in the northeast by the river Jayḥūn.

See Le Strange, *Lands*, 382–432; Bosworth, "Khurasan."

Khuwār al-Rayy (§4) a town east of Rayy, on the Khurasan road.

See Le Strange, *Lands*, 367.

Khwārazm (§§3, 5, 8–9, 24, 26, 71; Yāqūt §§3.3–3.4, 5.1–5.11) a region north of Khurasan, extending as far as the southern shore of the Caspian Sea, Khwārazm is used in the text also as the name of the region's capital, Kāth, the residence of the *khwārazm-shāh*.

See Le Strange, *Lands*, 446–59; Bosworth, "Kāth"; Bosworth, "Khʷārazm."

khwārazm-shāh (§8) the ancient Iranian title of the rulers of Khwārazm. The Khwārazm-Shāh dynasty ruled the area, remaining in power until the Mongol invasion. In Ibn Faḍlān's time the person holding this title was Muḥammad ibn ʿIrāq, who governed in the name of the Samanid emir.

See Bosworth, "Khʷārazm-Shāhs."

Kījlū (§36) the eighth river crossed by the caravan, on portable, collapsible camel-skin rafts, after its departure from Bajanāk territory.

Togan (*Reisebericht*, 34, n. 8) identifies it as the Kundurcha, pointing out the existence of a nearby village named Kijläw, on the lesser Cheremshan (see Kovalevskiĭ, *Kniga*, 192, n. 319). It is "Konjulû," according to Canard (*Voyage*, 49: see also 107, n. 138), and "Kunjulū," according to McKeithen (*Risālah*, 79, n. 217) and Lunde and Stone (*Ibn Fadlān*, 23, 226, n. 46). Frye (*Ibn Fadlān's Journey*, 97) identifies it as the modern "Kundurcha"; on Róna-Tas's map (*Hungarians and Europe*, 223), it is the Kundurcha.

Knāl (§36) the sixth river crossed by the caravan, on portable, collapsible camel-skin rafts, after its departure from Bajanāk territory.

Togan (*Reisebericht*, 34, n. 6) and Kovalevskiĭ (*Kniga*, 192, n. 317) read "Kināl" and identify it as the modern river Kinel. It is "Kinâl" according to Canard (*Voyage*, 49: see also 107, n. 138) and "Kināl," according to al-Dahhān (*Risālah*, 107, n. 6); McKeithen (*Risālah*, 78, n. 215), and Lunde and Stone (*Ibn Fadlān*, 23, 226, n. 46). Frye (*Ibn

Fadlān's Journey, 97) gives it as the modern "Kenel"; on Róna-Tas's map (*Hungarians and Europe*, 223) it is the Kinel.

kūdharkīn (§§24, 26, 29) the title given to any Ghuzziyyah noble who acts as deputy (*khalīfah* in the text) of the king of the Ghuzziyyah. There is no agreement on the meaning or etymology of the term. Togan (*Reisebericht*, 141) traces it to the Turkic phrase *kül erkin*.

See Canard, *Voyage*, 104, n. 100; McKeithen, *Risālah*, 62, n. 150; Lunde and Stone, *Ibn Fadlān*, 225, n. 38; Golden, *Introduction*, 209.

Kundur Khāqān (Yāqūt §4.4) the title given to the deputy of the *khāqān bih* among the Khazars.

Transcribed as "kundur khāqān" by Canard (*Voyage*, 85, 127, n. 342) and as "kundar" by McKeithen (*Risālah*, 154–55, n. 546) and Lunde and Stone (*Ibn Fadlān*, 55, 229, n. 88).

See Togan, *Reisebericht*, 260; Minorsky, *Ḥudūd al-ʿālam*, 323–24; Golden, *Khazar Studies*, 1:200–202; Golden, *Introduction*, 240.

Kūyabah (Yāqūt §4.3) Arabic name for the Rus' settlement of Kiev.

Līlī ibn Nuʿmān (§4) a Daylamī general who served the Caspian Zaydīs al-Ḥasan ibn ʿAlī al-Uṭrūsh and al-Ḥasan ibn Qāsim. The latter appointed him to the governorship of Jurjān. In early 309/921, just before the departure of the embassy, he had occupied al-Dāmghān and Nishapur but was captured and killed by the Samanid field marshal Ḥammawayh Kūsā in Rabiʿ al-Awwal, 309/July–August, 921, as the embassy was moving through Khurasan.

See Togan, *Reisebericht*, 5–6, n. 8; Canard, *Voyage*, 97, n. 21; McKeithen, *Risālah*, 32, n. 34.

Lesser Yināl see Yināl.

Mann (Yāqūt §5.9) a unit of weight common in Central Asia and Persia.

See Rebstock, "Islamic Weights and Measures," 2261.

Marw (§§4, 6, 31, 33) a town on Ibn Faḍlān's route between Sarakhs and Qushmahān, which was the source of some of the textiles presented by the embassy to local potentates.

See Le Strange, *Lands*, 397–403; Yakubovskii [Bosworth], "Marw al-Shāhidjān."

Muḥammad (§66) an alternate version of Ibn Faḍlān's given name Aḥmad. The Prophet Muḥammad was also known as Aḥmad (see Q Ṣaff 61:6).

Muḥammad ibn ʿIrāq see *khwārazm-shāh*.

Muḥammad ibn Sulaymān (§1; Yāqūt §§2.1, 3.1, 5.1, 6.1) the redoubtable secretary of the Army Bureau, who defeated the Qarmaṭians in Syria in 291/903, wrested Egypt from Ṭulunid control in 292/905, and had been trying to maintain order in the eastern empire. He died in the caliphal campaign against Aḥmad ibn ʿAlī, who had seized control of Rayy upon the assassination of the Abbasid governor, ʿAlī ibn Wahsudhān. His death would have meant that Ibn Faḍlān was without a principal patron, though Ibn Faḍlān seems also to have secured the patronage of the caliph in Baghdad. It was possible for a person to enjoy the patronage of more than one patron at the same time, though perhaps Ibn Faḍlān was a member of the caliph's household and functioned under the patronage of Muḥammad ibn Sulaymān.

See McKeithen, *Risālah*, 24, n. 2; Bonner, "The Waning of Empire," 339; Brett, "Egypt," 562–63.

Muqtadir, al- (§§1–3, 44; Yāqūt §§1.1, 1.3, 2.1, 3.1–3.2, 3.5, 4.1, 5.1, 6.1) the ruling caliph (r. 295–320/908–32) when Ibn Faḍlān's embassy made its journey. His full name was Abū l-Faḍl Jaʿfar ibn Aḥmad al-Muʿtaḍid, and his regnal title al-Muqtadir bi-llāh, "Mighty in God."

See van Berkel et al., *Crisis and Continuity at the Abbasid Court*.

musayyabī dinar (§§14, 31) the *musayyabī* was a coin of uncertain value said to have been minted in Transoxania by al-Musayyab, governor of Khurasan, especially common among Turkic peoples in northern Khwārazm. It is odd that they are described in the text as dinars, which were gold coins. Frye (*Ibn Fadlan's Journey*, 88–90) wonders whether Ibn Faḍlān is confusing "real *dinar*s or rare gold coins" with Khwarazmian coins and suggests that Ibn Faḍlān means "equivalents in value of so many *musayyabi* dirhams."

See Togan, *Reisebericht*, 111–13; Canard, *Voyage*, 102, n. 70; Frye, *Notes on the Early Coinage*, 29–31; Bosworth, "al-Ghiṭrīf b. ʿAṭāʾ."

Nadhīr al-Ḥaramī (§§3, 31, 41; Yāqūt §3.2) a powerful eunuch at al-Muqtadir's court. He presents the Bulghār king's letter to the caliph and organizes the finances of the mission. He is the *mawlā* (patron) of the caliph's envoy, Sawsan al-Rassī, and provides the mission with letters to Atrak, son of al-Qaṭaghān, the Ghuzziyyah military commander, and to the Bulghār king.

See Canard, *Voyage*, 95, n. 7, and McKeithen, *Risālah*, 26, n. 9, for references in Arabic sources.

Nahrawān (§4) the first town east of Baghdad reached by the mission after their departure.

See Le Strange, *Lands*, 61.

Naṣr ibn Aḥmad (§5) Naṣr (r. 301–31/914–23) became the Samanid emir of Khurasan as an eight-year-old boy. When Ibn Faḍlān visited him in 309/921 he would have been only fifteen or sixteen years old.

See Bosworth, "Naṣr b. Aḥmad b. Ismāʿīl."

Nishapur (§4) a town in Khurasan under Samanid control at the time of the mission.

See Le Strange, *Lands*, 382; Honigmann [Bosworth], "Nī<u>sh</u>āpūr."

pakand see *bakand*

Qaṭaghān, al- see Atrak, son of al-Qaṭaghān.

Qirmīsīn (§4) a town, modern Kermanshah, on Ibn Faḍlān's route between Ḥulwān and Hamadhān.

See Le Strange, *Lands*, 400.

Qushmahān (§4) a town on the edge of the Karakum desert, on Ibn Faḍlān's route between Marw and Baykand.

raṭl (§11; Yāqūt §5.8) a common, variable measure of weight.

See Ashtor, "Maḳāyil"; Hinz, *Islamische Masse*, 27–33.

Rayy (§4) an important town on the Khurasan road, between Hamadhān and Khuwār al-Rayy. At the time of the mission, it had been, for many years, the focus of the struggle for regional domination between the caliphate in Baghdad and the Samanids. Its ruins lie in the southern suburbs of present-day Tehran.

See Le Strange, *Lands*, 214–18; Minorsky, "Al-Rayy."

ruknī dinar (Yāqut §5.9) a gold coin of wide circulation in Khurasan and Central Asia.

Rūsiyyah (§§1, 72, 74–89; Yāqūt §§4.2–4.3, 6.1–6.10) also known in Arabic as *al-Rūs*, one of the marvels witnessed by Ibn Faḍlān while in the custody of the king of the Bulghārs, a mysterious group of traders and raiders that continues to fascinate more than a millennium after Ibn Faḍlān encountered them. Their identity in Arabic writings has long been debated, not least with regard to the homonymous state (known as Rus') that emerged during the fourth/tenth century. In Ibn Faḍlān's account, the Rūs are traders who set up camp on the bank of the Itil (Volga) and thus in or near Bulghār lands, and we are given a unique eyewitness description of their community.

Samanids a Persian dynasty, rulers of Transoxania and then of Khurasan (204–395/819–1005). At the time of the mission, the Samanid ruler, Naṣr ibn Aḥmad, acknowledged the suzerainty of the caliph and went by the title of "emir."

See Bosworth, "Sāmānids."

samarqandī dirham (§7) a specific type of coin said by Ibn Faḍlān to be made of yellow brass and to equal six *dānaq*s.

See also Frye, *Notes on the Coinage*, 29–31.

Ṣaqālibah (§§1, 2, 3, 8, 39, 66, 72; Yāqūt §§1.1, 2.1, 3.3-3.4, 4.1, 4.5, 5.1, 6.1) a name used in Arab-Islamic geographical and historical works, from the third/ninth century on, for certain northern peoples whose ethnic identity is not readily ascertainable. It may refer occasionally to Slavic peoples but seems generally to have a less specific connotation. At Yāqūt §4.5 it seems to denote the Finno-Ugrian peoples who live in the territories neighboring the Khazar realm. Throughout Ibn Faḍlān's account, the ruler of the Bulghārs is called the "king of the Ṣaqālibah" (§§1, 2, 3, 8, 39, 66, 72; Yāqūt §§2.1, 3.2, 3.4, 4.1, 5.1, 6.1).

Sarakhs (§§4, 6) a town on Ibn Faḍlān's route between Nishapur and Marw.

See Le Strange, *Lands*, 395–96; Bosworth, "Sara<u>kh</u>s."

Sāwah (§4) a caravan town (modern Saveh) on Ibn Faḍlān's route between Hamadhān and Rayy.

See Le Strange, *Lands*, 210–12; Minorsky [Bosworth] "Sāwa."

Sawsan al-Rassī (§§3, 42, 52; Yāqūt §§3.2, 3.4) eunuch and freedman, under the patronage of Nadhīr al-Ḥaramī; the most important member of the embassy, the envoy of the caliph.

Togan (*Reisebericht*, 3–4, n. 6) identifies him as Sawsan al-Jaṣṣāṣī. The name al-Jaṣṣāṣī indicates that he was a member of the household of Ibn al-Jaṣṣāṣ al-Jawharī. It was Sawsan al-Jaṣṣāṣī who betrayed Ibn al-Muʿtazz (d. 289/902), the caliph who ruled for a day, to al-Muqtadir's men.

Simnān (§4) a town (modern Semnan) some two hundred kilometers east of present-day Tehran, on Ibn Faḍlān's route between Khuwār al-Rayy and al-Dāmghān; at the time of the mission it was under Zaydī control.

See Le Strange, *Lands*, 366; Bosworth, "Simnān."

Sind (§61) the region around the lower course of the Indus river.

See Haig [Bosworth], "Sind."

Smwr (§36) the fifth river crossed by the caravan, on portable, collapsible camel-skin rafts, after its departure from Bajanāk territory.

Togan (*Reisebericht*, 34, n. 5) and Kovalevskiĭ (*Kniga*, 192, n. 316) identify it as the modern Samara, one of the major tributaries of the lower Volga. It is "Samûr," according to Canard (*Voyage*, 49: see also 107, n. 138), "Samūr," according to al-Dahhān (*Risālah*, 107, n. 5), McKeithen (*Risālah*, 78, n. 214), and Lunde and Stone (*Ibn Fadlān*, 23, 226, n. 46). Frye (*Ibn Fadlān's Journey*, 97) has "Samara"; on Róna-Tas's map (*Hungarians and Europe*, 223), it is the Samara.

Sūḥ (§36) the seventh river crossed by the caravan, on portable, collapsible camel-skin rafts, after its departure from Bajanāk territory.

Togan (*Reisebericht*, 34, n. 7) reads "Sūkh" and Kovalevskiĭ (*Kniga*, 192, n. 318) "Sūḥ." Both identify it as the modern Sok (or Soq, Suk). According to Canard, it is "Sûkh," (*Voyage*, 49,) and "Sâkh/Sokh" (*Voyage*, 107, n. 138). It is "Sūkh," according to al-Dahhān (*Risālah*, 107, n. 7), McKeithen (*Risālah*, 79, n. 216), and Lunde and Stone (*Ibn Fadlān*, 23, 226, n. 46). Frye (*Ibn Fadlān's Journey*, 97) identifies it as the modern "Sok"; on Róna-Tas's map (*Hungarians and Europe*, 223), it is the Sok.

Sujū, al- (§43; Yāqūt §3.4) apparently a honey drink—perhaps a kind of mead—drunk by the Bulghār king. The word is a transcription of *süčü*: Togan, *Reisebericht*, 44, n. 2; Róna-Tas, *Hungarians and Europe*, 226. There is disagreement about whether the drink is intoxicating or not: Canard, *Voyage*, 109, n. 156; al-Dahhān, *Risālah*, 116, n. 6; McKeithen, *Risālah*, 87, n. 254. Note, however, that Ibn Faḍlān does not say that he consumed this honey drink but that the king did. It is Yāqūt's quotation of the passage that adds the phrase *wa-sharabnā*, "and we drank too."

Ṣuʿlūk (§4) Muḥammad ibn ʿAlī Ṣuʿlūk, a Daylamī, the Samanid governor of Rayy from 289–304 to 912–16; brother of Aḥmad ibn ʿAlī and, at the time of the mission, the Abbasid governor of Rayy.

See Canard, *Voyage*, 96–97, n. 20; McKeithen, *Risālah*, 31, n. 28.

Suwāz (§69) name of a Bulghār clan whose members refuse to travel with the king, thus declaring their rejection of his conversion to Islam.

There is consensus that the *swān* of the Mashhad manuscript is a copyist's corruption of "Suwāz" (according to Kovalevskiĭ, *Kniga*, 222, n. 596, they were the ancestors of the Chuvash). The integration of the Suwāz into the Bulghārs was represented by the later settlement known as Suwār.

See Togan, *Reisebericht*, 203–10; Canard, *Voyage*, 116–17, n. 238; McKeithen, *Risālah*, 118, n. 369; Zimonyi, *Origins*, 42–45; Golden, *Introduction*, 255.

Ṭāgh (§§11, 17; Yāqūt §5.8) Togan (*Reisebericht*, 13) suggests that this is a tree of the amaranth genus *Haloxylon*, known by the Russian name *saxaul*. The saxaul ranges in size from a large shrub to a small tree, usually 2–8 meters tall. The wood is heavy and coarse and the bark spongy. The saxaul grows throughout the Middle East and Central Asia and is very hardy and drought-resistant. In addition to providing fuel for heating, the thick bark stores moisture, which may be squeezed out for drinking, making it an important source of water in arid regions.

See Kovalevskiĭ, *Kniga*, 173, n. 119.

Ṭāhir ibn ʿAlī (§4) Togan (*Reisebericht*, 6, n. 4) speculates that this may be Ṭāhir ibn ʿAlī al-Wazīr, who was in the service of Caliph al-Muktafī (r. 289–95/902–8).

Takīn al-Turkī (§§3, 8, 13, 16, 52, 68) a member of the caliphal embassy, presumably a "slave-soldier" of Turkic origin, who was very knowledgeable about the Turkic steppe peoples and the Volga Bulghārs. The local potentate of Khwārazm recognizes him as a prominent figure in the iron trade, which, in fourth/tenth-century terms, would also have implied that he worked as a weapons dealer.

Tekin (or *tegin*) was a title designating close familial relationship to a *khāqān*, usually a son or a brother, and was frequently used as a proper noun. The name is variously transcribed as "Takīn," by Togan (*Reisebericht*, 4, n. 1), "Tekin" or "Tegin," by Kovalevskiĭ (*Kniga*, 164, n. 33), "Tekîn," by Canard (*Voyage*, 28, 96, n. 11), "Tekīn," by McKeithen (*Risālah*, 28, n. 16), and "Tikīn," by Lunde and Stone (*Ibn Fadlān*, 4, 223, n. 11).

See Golden, *Khazar Studies*, 1:186–87.

Ṭanbūr (§83; Yāqūt §6.7) a long-necked stringed instrument from Central Asia.

Ṭarkhān (§33) the title of the most important member of the delegation of senior Ghuzziyyah figures convened by Atrak in order to consult about whether to permit the embassy to continue on its way.

Togan (*Reisebericht*, 30, n. 3) notes that this is a well-known Turkic title, especially among the Khazars. McKeithen (*Risālah*, 71, n. 187) states that "Ṭarkhān" is "a very ancient title indicating nobility . . . among Turks and Mongols."

See Golden, *Khazar Studies*, 1:210–13; Golden, *Introduction*, 209.

ṭāzijah (§9; Yāqūt §5.4) a coin used in Khwārazm.

See Togan, *Reisebericht*, 113–14; Canard, *Voyage*, 99, n. 48; Frye, *Notes on the Early Coinage*, 16–23; Frye, *Ibn Fadlān's Journey*, 88–90 (on the coins of Khwārazm).

Turk/Turks (§§1, 5, 12, 13, 15, 16, 18, 20, 23, 24, 26–30, 32, 37, 65; Yāqūt §§2.2, 4.3) a generic name for all the Turkic-speaking peoples of Central Asia with whom the Muslims came into contact. In the translation, I use "Turkic" for the language the Turks speak, and "Turkish" for their camels and yurts. I presume that by "Turkish camels" Ibn Faḍlān intends Bactrians.

Ūrm (§38) the third river crossed by the caravan after its departure from Bāshghird territory.

See Togan (*Reisebericht*, 37, n. 3). Kovalevskiĭ (*Kniga*, 194) suggests it is the modern river Urm. Today, there is a village with the name Urm where Volga Bulghar inscriptions have been found. It is omitted by Canard in his translation and note: *Voyage*, 51, 108, n. 145. It is "Ūram," according to al-Dahhān (*Risālah*, 110, n. 3) and McKeithen (*Risālah*, 81, n. 228), and "Uram/Urem," according to Lunde and Stone (*Ibn Fadlān*, 24, 226, n. 49). Frye (*Ibn Fadlān's Journey*, 97) identifies it as the modern "Urem"; it is not drawn on Róna-Tas's map (*Hungarians and Europe*, 223).

Ūrn (§38) the second river crossed by the caravan after its departure from Bāshghird territory.

Togan (*Reisebericht*, 37, n. 2) suggests it is the river Ürän, which enters the Volga across from modern Ulyanovsk. Near the Ürän is a Tatar village called Ürän-bashi (see Kovalevskiĭ, *Kniga*, 194). It is "Uran," according to Canard (*Voyage*, 51; see 108, n. 145), "Ūran," according to al-Dahhān (*Risālah*, 110, n. 2) and McKeithen (*Risālah*, 81, n. 227), and "Uran," according to Lunde and Stone (*Ibn Fadlān*, 24, 226, n. 49). Frye (*Ibn Fadlān's Journey*, 97), identifies it as the modern "Uran"; on Róna-Tas's map (*Hungarians and Europe*, 223), it is the Uren.

Wārsh (§34) the sixth river crossed by the caravan, on portable, collapsible camel-skin rafts, after its departure from Ghuzziyyah territory.

Togan (*Reisebericht*, 33, n. 1) and Kovalevskiĭ (*Kniga*, 192, n. 304) identify it as the modern Qaldagayti (or Kandagayti) river. It is to be read as "Wakhch," according to Canard (*Voyage*, 107, n. 134), who does not include it in his translation of the passage; "Wārsh," according to McKeithen (*Risālah*, 76, n. 201) and Lunde and Stone (*Ibn Fadlān*, 22, 226, n. 45); and "Warish," according to Frye (*Ibn Fadlān's Journey*, 42). Frye (*Ibn Fadlān's Journey*, 97) identifies it as the modern "Olenty or Kaldigayti."

Wbnā (§34) the eighth river crossed by the caravan, on portable, collapsible camel-skin rafts, after its departure from Ghuzziyyah territory.

Kovalevskiĭ (*Kniga*, 192, n. 306) identifies it as the Lesser Ankaty river (Sholek Antaky), which empties into Shalkar lake, in southern Kazakhstan. Togan (*Reisebericht*, 33, n. 3) suggests it may be read as "Wtbā" and correspond to the modern Utwa, which connects with the Ural river, but also points out that this would have been an unlikely detour for the embassy. It is the "Wtbā," according to al-Dahhān (*Risālah*, 106, n. 5), and the "Wabnâ," according to Canard (*Voyage*, 48, 107, n. 134), followed by McKeithen (*Risālah*, 76, n. 203) and Lunde and Stone (*Ibn Faḍlān*, 22, 226, n. 45). According to Frye (*Ibn Faḍlān's Journey*, 97), it is modern "Utba."

Wīsū (§§50, 65, 68; Yāqūt §1.2) according to the king of the Bulghārs, the Wīsū live three months' travel north of the Bulghārs and trade with them. Togan (*Reisebericht*, 55, n. 3) and Kovalevskiĭ (*Kniga*, 205, n. 475) agree that the Wīsū are the Veps.

See Göckenjan and Zimonyi, *Orientalische Berichte*, 261–62, ns. 85–95.

Wtīʿ (§38) the fifth river crossed by the caravan after its departure from Bāshghird territory.

Togan (*Reisebericht*, 37, n. 5) reads it as "Wtīgh" and identifies it as the Utka. It is "Watigh," according to Canard (*Voyage*, 51 and see 108, n. 145, where he reads "Watighla/Utka"); "Watīgh," according to al-Dahhān (*Risālah*, 110, n. 5), McKeithen (*Risālah*, 82, n. 230), and Lunde and Stone (*Ibn Faḍlān*, 25, 226, n. 49). Frye (*Ibn Faḍlān's Journey*, 97) identifies it as the modern "Utka." On Róna-Tas's map (*Hungarians and Europe*, 223), it is the Utka.

*W*rʿ* (§69) the name or title of a son-in-law of the Bulghār king, with whom the Suwāz clan ally themselves when they refuse to travel with the king and thus reject his conversion to Islam. According to Togan (*Reisebericht*, 75, n. 2), it is to be read "Wïyrïg" and reflects a Bulghār form of the ancient Turkic title *buyrug* (modern Turkish *buyruk*). Kovalevskiĭ (*Kniga*, 224, n. 604a) reads "Vyrag"; according to al-Dahhān (*Risālah*, 140, n. 7) and McKeithen (*Risālah*, 119, n. 372), it is to be transcribed as "Wīrigh" and, according to Lunde and Stone, as "Wīragh" (*Ibn Faḍlān*, 42 and 228, n. 75).

yabghū (§29) the regal title of the king of the Ghuzziyyah Turks.

See Togan, *Reisebericht*, 140–41; Canard, *Voyage*, 105, n. 113; al-Dahhān, *Risālah*, 101, n. 1; Frye, "Some Early Iranian Titles," 356–58; Golden, *Khazar Studies*, 1:187–90; Golden, *Introduction*, 209.

Yāqūt Yāqūt ibn ʿAbdallāh al-Rūmī al-Ḥamawī (d. 626/1229), a biographer and geographer renowned for his encyclopedic writings. "Al-Rūmī" ("the man from Rūm") refers to his Byzantine origin, and "al-Ḥamawī" connects him with Ḥamāh, in Syria. In his topographical dictionary *Kitab Muʿjam al-buldān*, he included quotations from Ibn Faḍlān's account, which remained the principal vestiges of the work until Togan's discovery of the Mashhad manuscript in 1923.

Yilghiz (§33) a member of the delegation of senior Ghuzziyyah figures convened by Atrak in order to consult about the embassy.

The word is variously transliterated "Baghliz" by Canard (*Voyage*, 47), followed by McKeithen (*Risālah*, 72 and n. 190) and Lunde and Stone (*Ibn Fadlān*, 21), "ʾĪlghz" by al-Dahhān (*Risālah*, 103), and "Ylgz (Yughrush?)" by Frye (*Ibn Fadlān's Journey*, 41).

See Golden, *Introduction*, 209.

yilik (Yāqūt §4.2) one of the titles of the vice-regent, that is, the non-khaganal ruler of the Khazars.

See Golden, *Khazar Studies*, 1:184–85; Golden, *Introduction*, 240; Róna-Tas, *Hungarians and Europe*, 233.

Yilṭawār (§§2, 44; Yāqūt §§3.2, 3.5) an arabicized form of the Turkic title *elteber*, written as *blṭwār* once in the Mashhad manuscript and in Yāqūt's quotation of the opening of the text. It seems to have been conferred on the Bulghār king or his father or both, presumably by the Khazars, to indicate a ruler subordinate to the Khazar *khāqān*.

Yināl (§§25, 33) apparently a title of a high-ranking Ghuzziyyah tribesman, used twice in the text. The first occurrence is qualified by the adjective *al-ṣaghīr* ("the younger" or "the lesser"), which may indicate age or status. It is possible that Ibn Faḍlān meets two men, the lesser Yināl (§25) and the Yināl (§33). The position of *yināl* is thought by some to designate the deputy of the *kūdharkīn* or the heir apparent to the *yabghū*.

The word is transcribed "Yināl" by McKeithen (*Risālah*, 63, n. 157), "Yanal" by Frye (*Ibn Fadlān's Journey*, 37), and "Ināl" by Lunde and Stone (*Ibn Fadlān*, 21, 226, n. 43).

See Golden, *Introduction*, 209.

Zamjān (§15) a garrison post, referred to as the Gate of the Turks, the first stopover taken by the embassy on leaving al-Jurjāniyyah, on the edge of the Ustyurt.

Zaydī/Zaydiyyah a branch of the Shi'ah, whose name comes from Zayd ibn 'Alī ibn al-Ḥusayn, who led a revolt in Kufa in 122/740. In Ibn Faḍlān's text, the Caspian (and not the Yemeni) Zaydiyyah are meant, in particular the group known as the Nāṣiriyyah, who accepted leadership from among the descendants of al-Ḥasan ibn 'Alī al-Uṭrūsh (d. 304/917), whose title was al-Nāṣir li-l-Ḥaqq, "he who brings victory to God's Truth."

See Madelung, "Zaydiyya."

Bibliography

Ashtor, E. “Maḳāyil, 1. In the Arabic, Persian and Turkish Lands.” In *Encyclopaedia of Islam*, 2nd ed. Leiden: Brill, 1991, 6:117–21.

Barthold, W. *Turkestan down to the Mongol Invasion*. Cambridge: Gibb, 2007.

———. [R. N. Frye]. “Bukhārā.” In *Encyclopaedia of Islam*, 2nd ed. Leiden: Brill, 1986: 1:1293–96.

Bonner, Michael. “The Waning of Empire, 861–945.” In *The New Cambridge History of Islam*. Vol. 1, *The Formation of the Islamic World Sixth to Eleventh Centuries*, edited by Chase F. Robinson, 305–59. Cambridge: Cambridge University Press, 2010.

Bosworth, C. E. “Al-Ghiṭrīf b. ʿAṭāʾ.” In *Encyclopaedia of Islam*, 2nd ed. Suppl. fasc. 5–6. Leiden: Brill, 1982, 326–27.

———. “Kāth.” In *Encyclopaedia of Islam*, 2nd ed. Leiden: Brill, 1997, 4:753–54.

———. “Khurāsān.” In *Encyclopaedia of Islam*, 2nd ed. Leiden: Brill, 1986, 5:55–59.

———. “Khʷārazm.” In *Encyclopaedia of Islam*, 2nd ed. Leiden: Brill, 1997, 4:1060–65.

———. “Khʷārazm-Shāhs.” In *Encyclopaedia of Islam*, 2nd ed. Leiden: Brill, 1997, 4:1065–68.

———. “Sāmānids. 1. History, Literary Life and Economic Activity.” In *Encyclopaedia of Islam*, 2nd ed. Leiden: Brill, 1995, 8:1025–29.

———. “Sarakhs.” In *Encyclopaedia of Islam*, 2nd ed. Leiden: Brill, 1997, 9:34.

———. "Simnān." In *Encyclopaedia of Islam*, 2nd ed. Leiden: Brill, 1997, 9:613–14.

———. "Naṣr b. Aḥmad b. Ismāʿīl." In *Encyclopaedia of Islam*, 2nd ed. Leiden: Brill, 1993, 7:1015.

Brett, Michael. "Egypt." In *The New Cambridge History of Islam*. Vol. 1, *The Formation of the Islamic World Sixth to Eleventh Centuries*, edited by Chase F. Robinson, 541–80. Cambridge: Cambridge University Press, 2010.

Bukharaev, R. *Islam in Russia: The Four Seasons*. Richmond: Curzon, 2000.

Canard, Marius. *Ibn Fadlân: Voyage chez les Bulgares de la Volga*. Paris: Sindbad, 1988.

Coetzee, J. M. *Waiting for the Barbarians*. London: Secker and Warburg, 1980.

Crone, P. "Mawlā." *In Encyclopaedia of Islam*, 2nd ed. Leiden: Brill, 1991, 6:874–82.

DeWeese, Devin. *Islamization and Native Religion in the Golden Horde*. University Park, PA: Pennsylvania State University Press, 1994.

Dunlop, D. M. *The History of the Jewish Khazars*. Princeton: Princeton University Press, 1954.

Duri, A. A. "Daskara." In *Encyclopaedia of Islam*, 2nd ed. Leiden: Brill, 1991, 2:165–66.

Edwards, P. *The Story of the Voyage: Sea-Narratives in Eighteenth-Century England*. Cambridge: Cambridge University Press, 1994.

Frye, Richard N. *Notes on the Early Coinage of Transoxania*. New York: American Numismatic Society, 1949.

———. "Some Early Iranian Titles." *Oriens* 15 (1962): 352–59.

———. "Hamadhān." In *Encyclopaedia of Islam*, 2nd ed. Leiden: Brill, 1986, 3:106–107.

———. *Ibn Fadlan's Journey to Russia: A Tenth-Century Traveler from Baghdad to the Volga River*. Princeton: Markus Wiener, 2005.

Göckenjan, Hansgerd, and Istvan Zimonyi. *Orientalische Berichte über die Völker Osteuropas und Zentralasiens im Mittelalter: Die Ǧayhānī-Tradition*. Wiesbaden: Harrassowitz, 2001.

Golden, P. B. "The Question of the Rus' Qağanate." *Archivum Eurasiae Medii Aevi* 2 (1982): 76–97.

———. *An Introduction to the History of the Turkic Peoples: Ethnogenesis and State-Formation in Medieval and Early Modern Eurasia and the Middle East.* Wiesbaden: Harrassowitz, 1992.

———. *Khazar Studies: An Historico-Philological Inquiry into the Origins of the Khazars.* Budapest: Akadémiai Kiadó, 1980.

Greenblatt, Stephen. *Marvelous Possessions: The Wonder of the New World.* Oxford: Clarendon Press, 1991.

Haig, T. W. [C. E. Bosworth]. "Sind. 1. History in the pre-Modern Period." In *Encyclopaedia of Islam*, 2nd ed. Leiden: Brill, 1997, 9:632–35.

Hill, Christopher. *The English Bible and the Seventeenth Century Revolution.* London: Penguin, 1994.

Hill, D. R. "Sāʿa." *In Encyclopaedia of Islam*, 2nd ed. Leiden: Brill, 1995, 8:654–56.

Hinz, W. *Islamische Masse und Gewichte.* Leiden: Brill, 1970.

———. "Farsakh." In *Encyclopaedia of Islam*, 2nd ed. Leiden: Brill, 1991, 2:812–13.

Honigmann, E. [C. E. Bosworth]. "Nīshāpūr." In *Encyclopaedia of Islam*, 2nd ed. Leiden: Brill, 1995, 8:62–64.

Ibn Faḍlān, Aḥmad. *Risālat Ibn Faḍlān.* Edited by Sāmī al-Dahhān. Damascus: al-Majmaʿ al-ʿIlmī al-ʿArabī, 1959.

Ibn Rustah. *Kitāb al-Aʿlāq al-nafīsah.* Edited by M. J. de Goeje. Leiden: Brill, 1967.

Iṣṭakhrī, al-. *Kitāb Masālik al-mamālik.* Edited by M. J. de Goeje. Leiden: Brill, 1967.

Kennedy, Hugh. *The Prophet and the Age of the Caliphates.* London: Longman, 1991.

Kipling, Rudyard. *The Man Who Would Be King: Selected Stories of Rudyard Kipling.* London: Penguin, 2011.

Klyashtornyj, S. G. "The Oguz of the Central Asia and the Guzs of the Aral region." *International Journal of Central Asian Studies* 2 (1997): 1–4.

Kovalevskiĭ, A. P. *Kniga Akhmeda Ibn Faḍlāna o ego puteshestvii na Volgu 921–2.* Kharkiv: Izdatelstvo Gos. Universiteta, 1956.

Lambton, A. K. S. "Kirmānshāh." In *Encyclopaedia of Islam*, 2nd ed. Leiden: Brill, 1986, 5:167–71.

Le Strange, Guy. *The Lands of the Eastern Caliphate*. Cambridge: Cambridge University Press, 1930.

Lockhart, L. "Ḥulwān." In *Encyclopaedia of Islam*, 2nd ed. Leiden: Brill, 1986, 3:571–72.

Lunde, Paul, and Caroline Stone. *Ibn Fadlān and the Land of Darkness: Arab Travellers in the Far North*. London: Penguin, 2012.

Macintyre, Ben. *Josiah the Great: The True Story of the Man Who Would Be King*. London: HarperCollins, 2004.

Madelung, W. "The Minor Dynasties of Northern Iran." In *The Cambridge History of Iran*. Vol. 4, *The Period from the Arab Invasion to the Saljuqs*, edited by R. N. Frye, 198–249. Cambridge: Cambridge University Press, 1999.

———. "Zaydiyya." In *Encyclopaedia of Islam*, 2nd ed. Leiden: Brill, 2002, 11:477–81.

Markwart, J. "Ein arabischer Bericht über die arktischen (uralischen) Länder aus dem 10. Jahrhundert." *Ungarische Jahrbücher* 4 (1924): 261–334.

Massignon, Louis. *Hallāj. Mystic and Martyr*. Translated, edited, and abridged by Herbert Mason. Princeton: Princeton University Press, 1994.

———. [L. Gardet]. "al-Ḥallādj." In *Encyclopaedia of Islam*. 2nd ed. Leiden: Brill, 1986, 3:99–104.

———. "Ḥāmid b. al-ʿAbbās." In *Encyclopaedia of Islam*. 2nd ed. Leiden: Brill, 1986, 3:133.

Masʿūdī, Abū l-Ḥasan al-. *Murūj al-dhahab wa-maʿādin al-jawhar*. Edited by Charles Pellat. 7 vols. Beirut: Manshūrāt al-Jāmiʿah al-Lubnāniyyah, 1965.

McKeithen, J. E. *The Risālah of Ibn Faḍlān: An Annotated Translation with Introduction*. PhD diss., Indiana University, 1979.

Miles, G. C. "Dīnār." In *Encyclopaedia of Islam*, 2nd ed. Leiden: Brill, 1991, 2:297–99.

———. "Dirham." In *Encyclopaedia of Islam*, 2nd ed. Leiden: Brill, 1991, 2:319–20.

Minorsky, V. *Ḥudūd al-ʿālam*. Edited by C. E. Bosworth. Cambridge: Gibb, 1982.

———. [C. E. Bosworth]. "Al-Rayy, 1. History." In *Encyclopaedia of Islam*, 2nd ed. Leiden: Brill, 1995, 8:471–73.

———. [C. E. Bosworth]. "Sāwa, 1. History." In *Encyclopaedia of Islam*, 2nd ed. Leiden: Brill, 1997, 9:85–87.

Miskawayh. *Tajārib al-umam*. Edited by Abū l-Qāsim Imāmī. Tehran: Dār Surūsh li-l-Ṭibāʿah wa-l-Nashr, 2001.

Monnot, G. "Ṣalāt, 3.A. The Five Daily Prayers." In *Encyclopaedia of Islam*, 2nd ed. Leiden: Brill, 1995, 8:928–29.

Noonan, T. S. "Some Observations on the Economy of the Khazar Khaganate." In *The World of the Khazars: New Perspectives: Selected Papers from the Jerusalem 1999 International Conference*, edited by P. B. Golden, H. Ben-Shammai, and A. Róna-Tas, 207–44. Leiden: Brill, 2007.

Pellat, Ch. "Al-Djayhānī." In *Encyclopaedia of Islam*, Suppl. fasc. 5–6. Leiden: Brill, 1982, 265–66.

Rebstock, Ulrich. "Islamic Weights and Measures." In *Encyclopaedia of the History of Science, Technology and Medicine in Non-Western Cultures*, edited by Helaine Seline, 2255–67. Berlin: Springer, 2008.

Rekaya, M. "Ḳārinids." In *Encyclopaedia of Islam*, 2nd ed. Leiden: Brill, 1997, 4:644–47.

Riley-Smith, J. "The State of Mind of Crusaders to the East, 1095–1300." In *The Oxford Illustrated History of the Crusades*, edited by J. Riley-Smith, 66–90. Oxford: Oxford University Press, 1997.

Ritter, Hellmut. "Zum Text von Ibn Faḍlān's Reisebericht." *Zeitschrift der Deutschen Morgendländischen Gesellschaft* 96 (1942): 98–126.

Róna-Tas, A. *Hungarians and Europe in the Early Middle Ages*. Budapest: Central European University Press, 1999.

Shaban, M. A. *Islamic History: A New Interpretation*. Vol. 2, A.D. 750–1055 (A.H. 132–448). Cambridge: Cambridge University Press, 1981.

Sourdel, D. "Ghulām, 1. The Caliphate." In Encyclopaedia of Islam, 2nd ed. Leiden: Brill, 1991, 2:1079–81.

Spuler, B. "Āmū Darya." In *Encyclopaedia of Islam*, 2nd ed. Leiden: Brill, 1986, 1:454–57.

Spuler, B. "Gurgandj." In *Encyclopaedia of Islam*, 2nd ed. Leiden: Brill, 1986, 3:1141–42.

Strothmann, R. "Al-Ḥasan al-Uṭrūsh." In *Encyclopaedia of Islam*, 2nd ed. Leiden: Brill, 1986, 3:254–55.

Subrahmanyam, Sanjay. *The Career and Legend of Vasco da Gama*. Cambridge: Cambridge University Press, 1997.

Tanūkhī, al-Muḥassin ibn ʿAlī al-. *Nishwār al-muḥādarah wa-akhbār al-mudhākarah*. Edited by ʿAbbūd al-Shaljī. 8 vols. Beirut: Dār Ṣādir, 1971.

Togan, A. Zeki Velidi. *Ibn Faḍlān's Reisebericht*. Abhandlungen für die Kunde des Morgenlandes 24, no. 3. Leipzig: Brockhaus, 1939.

van Berkel, M. *Accountants and Men of Letters. Status and Position of Civil Servants in Early Tenth Century Baghdad*. PhD diss., Amsterdam University, 2003.

van Berkel, Maaike, Nadia El Cheikh, Hugh Kennedy, and Letizia Osti, eds. *Crisis and Continuity at the Abbasid Court: Formal and Informal Politics in the Caliphate of al-Muqtadir (295–320/908–32)*. Leiden: Brill, 2013.

von Denffer, Ahmad. *ʿUlūm al-Qurʾān. An Introduction to the Sciences of the Qurʾān*, 2nd ed. Markfield: The Islamic Foundation, 2003.

Yāqūt al-Ḥamawī al-Rūmī. *Kitāb Muʿjam al-buldān*, edited by F. Wüstenfeld. Leipzig: Brockhaus, 1866.

Yakubovskii, A. Y. [C. E. Bosworth]. "Marw al-Shāhidjān." In *Encyclopaedia of Islam*, 2nd ed. Leiden: Brill, 1991, 6:618–21.

Zamora, Margarita. "Christopher Columbus's 'Letter to the Sovereigns:' Announcing the Discovery." In New World Encounters, edited by Stephen Greenblatt, 1–10. Berkeley: University of California Press, 1993.

Zettersteen, K. V. [C. E. Bosworth]. "Al-Muktadir." In *Encyclopaedia of Islam*, 2nd ed. Leiden: Brill, 1993, 7:541–42.

———. [C. E. Bosworth]. "Al-Muktafī." In *Encyclopaedia of Islam*, 2nd ed. Leiden: Brill, 1993: 7:542–43.

Zimonyi, I. *The Origins of the Volga Bulghars*. Szeged: Attila József University, 1990.

Further Reading

Works prefixed with an asterisk are either popular writings or useful overviews from which those unfamiliar with the subject might benefit. Readers should look out for the publication of *Muslims on the Volga in the Viking Age*, edited by Jonathan Shepherd and Luke Treadwell, proceedings of the important Oxford 2016 conference "Ibn Faḍlān and the Great Unwashed." This volume will provide a comprehensive companion to my translation.

Reproduction of the Mashhad Manuscript

Majmūʿ fī l-jughrāfiyā: mimmā allafahu Ibn al-Faqīh wa-Ibn Faḍlān wa-Abū Dulaf al-Khazrajī. Edited by Fuat Sezgin, with M. Amawi, C. Ehrig-Eggert, and E. Neubauer. Frankfurt am Main: Institute for the History of Arabic-Islamic Science at the Johann Wolfgang Goethe University, 1994 [additional photographic reproductions are to be found in Kovalevskiĭ, *Kniga*, and Czeglédy, *Zur Meschheder Handschrift*].

Editions of the *Kitāb*

Togan, A. Zeki Velidi. *Ibn Faḍlān's Reisebericht.* Abhandlungen für die Kunde des Morgenlandes 24, no. 3. Leipzig: Brockhaus, 1939 (a classic of twentieth-century scholarship, containing an edition and extensive and detailed commentary).

Risālat Ibn Faḍlān. Edited by Sāmī al-Dahhān. Damascus: al-Majmaʿ al-ʿIlmī al-ʿArabī, 1959.

Riḥlat Ibn Faḍlān. Edited by Ḥaydar Muḥammad Ghaybah. Beirut: al-Sharikah al-ʿĀlamiyyah li-l-Kitāb, 1994.

Risālat Ibn Faḍlān. Edited by Shakīr Lu'aybī. Abu Dhabi and Beirut: Dār al-Suwaydī li-l-Nashr wa-l-Tawzī' and al-Mu'assasah al-'Arabīyah li-l-Dirāsāt wa-l-Nashr, 2003.

Selected Translations of the *Kitāb*

Danish

Simonsen, J. B. *Vikingerne ved Volga: Ibn Faḍlāns rejsebeskrivelse*. Højberg: Wormianum, 1997 [a partial translation].

English

McKeithen, J. E. *The Risālah of Ibn Faḍlān: An Annotated Translation with Introduction*. PhD diss., Indiana University, 1979.

*Frye, Richard N. *Ibn Fadlan's Journey to Russia: A Tenth-Century Traveler from Baghdad to the Volga River*. Princeton: Markus Wiener, 2005.

*Lunde, Paul, and Caroline Stone. *Ibn Fadlān and the Land of Darkness: Arab Travellers in the Far North*. London: Penguin, 2012.

French

Canard, Marius. *Ibn Fadlân: Voyage chez les Bulgares de la Volga*. Paris: Sindbad, 1988. First published as "La Relation du Voyage d'Ibn Fadlân chez les Bulgares," *Annales de l'Institut d'Études Orientales* 5 (1958): 41–145.

*Charles-Dominique, Paul. *Voyageurs arabes: Ibn Faḍlân, Ibn Jubayr, Ibn Baṭṭûṭa et un auteur anonyme*. Paris: Gallimard, 1995.

German

Fraehn, C. M. *Ibn Fozlan's und andere Araber Berichte über die Russen älterer Zeit*. St. Petersburg: Kaiserl. Akademie der Wissenschaften, 1823.

Togan, A. Zeki Velidi. *Ibn Faḍlān's Reisebericht*. Abhandlungen für die Kunde des Morgenlandes 24, no. 3. Leipzig: Brockhaus, 1939.

Norwegian

Birkeland, Harris. *Nordens Historie i Middelalderen etter Arabiske Kilder*. Oslo: Jacob Dybwad, 1954 [a partial translation].

Persian

Ṭabāṭabā'ī, Abū l-Fażl. *Safarnāmah az Aḥmad ibn Fażlān ibn al-ʿAbbās ibn Rāshid ibn Ḥammād.* Manābiʿ-i tārīkh va-jughrāfiyā-yi Īrān 2. Tehran: Intishārāt-i Bunyād-i Farhang-i Īrān, 1966.

Polish

Kmietowicz, A., F. Kmietowicz, and T. Lewicki. *Źródła arabskie do dziejów słowiańszczyzny.* Wroclaw: Zakład im. Ossolińskich, 1985 [edition, translation, and commentary].

Russian

Kratchkovskiĭ, I. *Puteshestvie Ibn-Fadlana na Volgu.* Moscow and Leningrad: Izdatelstvo Akademii Nauk SSSR, 1939 [translation, with notes and commentary, under the general editorship of Kratchkovskiĭ].

Kovalevskiĭ, A. P. *Kniga Akhmeda Ibn Faḍlāna o ego puteshestvii na Volgu 921–2.* Kharkiv: Izdatelstvo Gos. Universiteta, 1956 [also contains a commentary and a facs. reprod. of the Mashhad manuscript].

Kuleshova, V. S. "Kniga Akhmada ibn Fadlana Perevod s arabskogo i primechaniya." In *Ibn Faḍlān's Journey: Volga Route from Baghdad to Bulghar.* Moscow: Mardjani Publishing House, 2016.

Collections of Articles

The following books contain many articles that will be of interest to those wanting to know more about Ibn Faḍlān, or the Turkic world of the period, or the tradition of Arabic geographical writing.

Bosworth, C. E., ed. *The Turks in the Early Islamic World.* Aldershot UK and Burlington VT: Ashgate, 2007.

Golden, Peter B. *Nomads and their Neighbours in the Russian Steppe: Turks, Khazars and Qipchaqs.* Aldershot: Variorum, 2003.

———. *Turks and Khazars: Origins, Institutions, and Interactions in Pre-Mongol Eurasia.* Aldershot: Variorum, 2010.

Golden, Peter B., H. Ben-Shammai, and A. Róna-Tas, eds. *The World of the Khazars: New Perspectives*. Selected Papers from the Jerusalem 1999 International Conference. Leiden: Brill, 2007.

Khazanov, Anatoly M., and Andre Wink, eds. *Nomads in the Sedentary World*. Richmond: Curzon, 2000.

Netton, I. R., ed. *Islamic and Middle Eastern Travellers and Geographers*. London: Routledge, 2007.

Noonan, T. S. *The Islamic World, Russia and the Vikings, 750–900: The Numismatic Evidence*. Aldershot: Variorum, 1998.

Sezgin, F., with M. Amawi, C. Ehrig-Eggert, and E. Neubauer, eds. *Texts and Studies on the Historical Geography and Topography of Northern and Eastern Europe*, vol. 3. Frankfurt am Main: Institute for the History of Arabic-Islamic Science at the Johann Wolfgang Goethe University, 1994.

On Ibn Faḍlān and his *Kitāb*

Bosworth, C. E. "Aḥmad. b. Fażlān." In *Encyclopaedia Iranica*. London: Routledge and Kegan Paul, 1985, 1:640.

Canard, M. "Ibn Faḍlān." In *Encyclopaedia of Islam*, 2nd ed. Leiden: Brill, 1986, 3:759.

Czeglédy, K. "Zur Meschheder Handschrift von Ibn Faḍlān's Reisebericht." *Acta Orientalia* 1 (1950–51): 217–43.

Dunlop, D. M. "Zeki Validi's Ibn Faḍlān." *Die Welt des Orients* 1 (1947–52): 307–12.

Frye, R. N., and R. P. Blake. "Notes on the Risala of Ibn-Fadlan." *Byzantina Metabyzantina* 1, no. 2 (1949): 7–37 [repr. in *The Turks in the Early Islamic World*, edited by C. E. Bosworth, 229–59, Aldershot UK and Burlington VT, Ashgate, 2007].

*Gabriel, J. "Among the Norse Tribes: The Remarkable Account of Ibn Fadlan." *Aramco World* 50, no. 6 (1999): 36–42.

Graf, H.-J. "Die Bedeutung des Ibn Faḍlān für die germanische Altertumskunde." In *Zeki Velidi Togan'a Armağan. Symbolae in honorem Z.V. Togan*, 397–404. Istanbul: Maarif Basımevi, 1950–55.

Kowalska, M. "Ibn Faḍlān's Account of His Journey to the State of the Bulġārs." *Folia Orientalia* 14 (1972–73): 219–30.

Manylov, Y. P. "O puti Ibn Faḍlāna iz Khorezma cherez Plato Ustyurt [On Ibn Faḍlān's route from Khorezm through Plato (sic) Ust Yurt]." *Sovetskaya Arkheologiya* 2 (1979): 92–100.

Miquel, André. *La géographie humaine du monde musulman jusqu'au milieu du XIe siècle: Géographie et géographie humaine dans la littérature arabe des origines à 1050*, Paris and The Hague: Mouton, 1967 [especially relevant is the discussion of Ibn Faḍlān on pp. 132–39].

Montgomery, J. E. "Pyrrhic Scepticism and the Conquest of Disorder: Prolegomenon to the Study of Ibn Faḍlān." In *Problems in Arabic Literature*, edited by M. Maroth, 43–89. Piliscsaba: The Avicenna Institute of Middle Eastern Studies, 2004.

———. "Travelling Autopsies: Ibn Faḍlān and the Bulghār." *Middle Eastern Literatures* 7, no. 1 (2004): 3–32.

———. "Spectral Armies, Snakes, and a Giant from Gog and Magog: Ibn Faḍlān as Eyewitness Among the Volga Bulghars." *The Medieval History Journal* 9 (2006): 63–87.

Ritter, H. "Zum Text von Ibn Faḍlān's Reisebericht." *Zeitschrift der Deutschen Morgenländischen Gesellschaft* 96 (1942): 98–126.

Safwat, N. F. "The First Arab Diplomatic Envoy to Russia from Baghdad." *Ur* 2 (1981): 10–18.

Sobolevskii, A. I. "Zápiska Ibn-Faḍlāna [Le mémoire d'Ibn-Faḍlān]." *Comptes rendus de l'Académie des sciences de Russie, B* (1929): 223–27.

Zakhoder, B. N. "Ibn Faḍlān i al-Masʿūdī." *Kratkie Soobshcheniya Instituta Vostokovedeniya* 38 (1960): 15–18.

Al-Muqtadir's Reign and Early Fourth/Tenth-Century Administration

van Berkel, M. *Accountants and Men of Letters. Status and Position of Civil Servants in Early Tenth Century Baghdad*. PhD diss., Amsterdam University, 2003.

van Berkel, Maaike, Nadia El Cheikh, Hugh Kennedy, and Letizia Osti, eds. *Crisis and Continuity at the Abbasid Court: Formal and Informal Politics in the Caliphate of al-Muqtadir (295–320/908–32)*. Leiden: Brill, 2013.

Zetterstéen, K. V. [C. E. Bosworth]. "Al-Muḳtadir." In *Encyclopaedia of Islam*, 2nd ed. Leiden: Brill, 1993, 7:541–42.

Geography and Routes

To acquire a sense of the geography and itineraries mentioned in Ibn Faḍlān's account, the following studies, arranged according to the route of the mission, are useful:

Le Strange, Guy. *The Lands of the Eastern Caliphate*. Cambridge: Cambridge University Press, 1930 [an indispensable gazetteer for the topography of the route from Baghdad to the Ustyurt].

Minorsky, V. [C. E. Bosworth]. "Al-Rayy." In *Encyclopaedia of Islam*, 2nd ed. Leiden: Brill, 1995, 8:471–73.

Bosworth, C. E. "Khurāsān." In *Encyclopaedia of Islam*. 2nd ed., Leiden: Brill, 1986, 5:55–59.

Barthold, W. [R. N. Frye]. "Bukhārā." In *Encyclopaedia of Islam*, 2nd ed. Leiden: Brill, 1986, 2:1293–96.

Bosworth, C. E. "Khʷārazm." In *Encyclopaedia of Islam*. 2nd ed, Leiden: Brill, 1997, 4:1060–65.

Spuler, B. "Gurgandj." In *Encyclopaedia of Islam*. 2nd ed, Leiden: Brill, 1991, 2:1141–42.

Planhol, X. de. "Caspian Sea." In *Encyclopaedia of Iran*. Costa Mesa: Maza, 1992, 5:48–61.

Róna-Tas, A. *Hungarians and Europe in the Early Middle Ages*. Budapest: Central European University Press, 1999 [on p. 223, there is a detailed map of Ibn Faḍlān's reconstructed riverine route from Ghuzziyyah territory to Bulghār].

Spuler, B. "Itil." In *Encyclopaedia of Islam*. 2nd ed, Leiden: Brill, 1997, 4:280–81.

On Trade and Trade Routes

Ducène, J.-Ch. "Le commerce des fourrures entre l'Europe orientale et le Moyen-Orient à l'époque médiévale (IXe-XIIIe siècle): pour une perspective historique." *Acta Orientalia* 58, no. 2 (2005): 215–28.

Kovalev, R. "The Infrastructure of the Northern Part of the 'Fur Road' between the Middle Volga and the East during the Middle Ages." *Archivum Eurasiae Medii Aevi* 11 (2000–1): 25–64 [deals specifically with the part of the trade route traversed by Ibn Faḍlān, from Khwārazm to Bulghār on the Volga].

*Martin, Janet. *Treasure of the Land of Darkness: The Fur Trade and its Significance for Medieval Russia.* Cambridge: Cambridge University Press, 1986.

Peoples and Tribes in the *Kitāb*

The territories north of the caliphate, from the realm of the Samanids east of the Caspian to Bulghār on the middle Volga, are not well documented for the period in question. They were inhabited predominantly by nomadic or semi-nomadic Turkic tribes, and large-scale migrations were frequent. In the early fourth/tenth century an important trade route emerged between the Samanids and the Bulghārs of the middle Volga, along which caravans transported great quantities of goods in exchange for Arabic silver dirhams, some of which were produced specifically for export via this trading relationship.

*Christian, David. *A History of Russia, Central Asia and Mongolia.* Vol. 1, *Inner Eurasia from Prehistory to the Mongol Empire.* Oxford: Blackwell, 1998 [a useful historical overview with a section on the Samanids].

Dolukhanov, Pavel. *The Early Slavs: Eastern Europe from the Initial Settlement to the Kievan Rus.* London and New York: Longman, 1996 [valuable archaeological study].

*Frye, Richard N. *The Golden Age of Persia*, London: Orion, 2000.

Göckenjan, Hansgerd, and Istvan Zimonyi. *Orientalische Berichte über die Völker Osteuropas und Zentralasiens im Mittelalter: Die*

Ǧayhānī-Tradition. Wiesbaden: Harrassowitz, 2001 [analyzes and discusses texts by other Arabic writers on some of the peoples encountered by Ibn Faḍlān].

*Golden, Peter B. *An Introduction to the History of the Turkic Peoples: Ethnogenesis and State-Formation in Medieval and Early Modern Eurasia and the Middle East.* Wiesbaden: Harrassowitz, 1992 [essential reading].

*———. *Central Asia in World History.* New York: Oxford University Press, 2011 [the best place to start for an overview of the region, from ancient to modern].

Khazanov, A. *Nomads and the Outside World.* Madison: University of Wisconsin Press, 1994.

Minorsky, V. *Ḥudūd al-ʿālam.* Edited by C. E. Bosworth. Cambridge: Gibb, 1982 [a translation of this important early anonymous Persian geography, with excellent commentary].

Pritsak, O. "The Turcophone Peoples in the Area of the Caucasus from the Sixth to the Eleventh Century." In *Il Caucaso: Cerniera fra culture dal Mediterraneo alla Persia (secoli IV–XI) 20–26 aprile 1995*, vol. 1, 223–45. Spoleto: Sede dello Centro, 1996.

Sinor, Denis. *Introduction à l'étude de l'Eurasie Centrale.* Wiesbaden: Harrassowitz, 1963 [a useful if outdated bibliographic resource].

*———, ed. *The Cambridge History of Early Inner Asia*, Cambridge: Cambridge University Press, 1990 [excellent survey articles on the Turkic peoples of the steppes].

*Soucek, S. *A History of Inner Asia*, Cambridge: Cambridge University Press, 2000.

Roux, J.-P. *La mort chez les peuples altaïques anciens et médiévaux.* Paris: Librairie d'Amérique et d'Orient, 1963.

———. *Faune et flore sacrées dans les societés altaïques.* Paris: Librairie d'Amérique et d'Orient, 1966.

———. "Tengri." In *The Encyclopedia of Religion.* New York: MacMillan, 1987, 14:401–3.

———. "Turkic Religions." In *The Encyclopedia of Religion.* New York: MacMillan, 1987, 15: 87–94.

Shboul, A. M. H. *Al-Masʿūdī and His World: A Muslim Humanist and His Interest in Non-Muslims*. London: Ithaca Press, 1979 [al-Masʿūdī's work of human geography, dating from several decades after Ibn Faḍlān's mission, provides notices on many of the peoples and places Ibn Faḍlān visited].

*Whittow, Mark. *The Making of Byzantium, 600–1025*. Berkeley and Los Angeles: University of California Press, 1996 [excellent account of Byzantium's dealings with many of the peoples encountered by Ibn Faḍlān].

The Ghuzziyyah

The Ghuzziyyah (Ghuzz/Oghuz) were an important Turkic tribe, whose earliest recorded abode was northeast of the Caspian Sea. In the fourth/tenth century they began moving west into the Khazar realm and ultimately played a role in its downfall.

Adamović, M. "Die alten Oghusen." *Materialia Turcica* 7–8 (1981–82): 26–50.

Agajanov, S. G. "The States of the Oghuz, the Kimek and the Kïpchak." In *History of Civilizations of Central Asia*. Vol. 4, *The Age of Achievement: AD 750 to the End of the Fifteenth Century. Part One, The Historical, Social and Economic Setting.*, edited by M. S. Asimov and C. E. Bosworth, 61–76. Paris: Unesco, 1998.

Cahen, Cl. "Ghuzz." In *Encyclopaedia of Islam*, 2nd ed. Leiden: Brill, 1991, 2:1106–10.

Golden, P. B. "The Migrations of the Oğuz." *Archivum Ottomanicum* 4 (1972): 45–84 [reprinted as Article IV in his *Nomads and Their Neighbours*].

Gömeç, S. "The Identity of Oguz Kagan. The Oguz in the History and the Epics of Oguz Kagan." *Oriente Moderno* 89, no. 1 (2009): 57–66.

Gündüz, T. "Oguz-Turkomans." In *The Turks*. Vol. 1, *Early Ages*, edited by Hasan Celâl Güzel, C. Cem Oğuz, and Osman Karatay, 463–75. Ankara: Yeni Türkiye, 2002.

Husseinov, R. "Les sources syriaques sur les croyances et les moeurs des Oghuz du VIIe au XIII siècle." *Turcica* 8, no. 1 (1976): 21–27.

Koca, S. "The Oghuz (Turkoman) Tribe Moving from Syr Darya (Jayhun) Region to Anatolia." In *The Turks*. Vol. 2, *Middle Ages*, edited by Hasan Celâl Güzel, C. Cem Oğuz, and Osman Karatay, 129–43. Ankara: Yeni Türkiye, 2002.

Klyashtornyj, S. G. "The Oguz of Central Asia and the Guzs of the Aral region." *International Journal of Central Asian Studies* 2 (1997): 1–4.

Salgado, F. M. "El Arabismo Algoz (al-guzz): contenido y uso." *Historia, Instituciones, Documentos* 26 (1999): 319–28.

Nagrodzka-Majchrzyk, T. "Les Oghouz dans la relation d'Aḥmad Ibn Faḍlān." *Rocznik Orientalistyczny* 49, no. 2 (1994): 165–69.

Zachariadou, E. A. "The Oğuz Tribes: The Silence of the Byzantine Sources." In *Itinéraires d'Orient: Hommages à Claude Cahen*, edited by R. Curiel and R. Gyselen, 285–89. Bures-sur-Yvette: Groupe pour l'Étude de la Civilisation du Moyen-Orient, 1994.

The Bajanāk

The Bajanāk (Pechenegs) were a nomadic or semi-nomadic Turkic people first reported east of the Caspian Sea. In the third/ninth century they migrated west, under pressure from the Ghuzziyyah (Ghuzz/Oghuz). As allies of the Byzantines, the Pechenegs were an important force on the Pontic steppes and further west, near Kievan Rus', and, by the end of the century, they had driven the Magyars to the Pannonian lowlands, where the state of Hungary was established.

Romashov, S. A. "The Pechenegs in Europe in the Ninth-Tenth Centuries." *Rocznik Orientalistyczny* 52, no. 1 (1999): 21–35.

Takács, B. Z. "Khazars, Pechenegs and Hungarians in the Ninth Century." In *The Turks*. Vol. 1, *Early Ages*, edited by Hasan Celâl Güzel, C. Cem Oğuz, and Osman Karatay, 524–32. Ankara: Yeni Türkiye, 2002.

Wozniak, F. E. "Byzantium, the Pechenegs, and the Rus': The Limitations of a Great Power's Influence on its Clients in the Tenth Century Eurasian Steppe." *Archivum Eurasiae Medii Aevi* 4 (1984): 299–316.

The Bāshghird

Not much is known about the Bāshghird (Bashkirs) in the fourth/tenth century, although they are mentioned by several Arab geographers. They were apparently an independent people occupying territories on both sides of the Ural mountain range in the region of the Volga, Kama, and Tobol Rivers.

Togan, Z. V. "Bashdjirt." In *Encyclopaedia of Islam*, 2nd ed. Leiden: Brill, 1986, 1:1075–77.

The Bulghār

The Turkic Volga Bulghārs established their state on the confluence of the Volga and Kama rivers in the third/ninth century. Early in the fourth/tenth century they entered into a dynamic trading relationship with the Samanids in Central Asia, as a result of which the territory of the Volga Bulghārs became one of the principal emporia of the period, rivaling and ultimately outlasting those of the Khazars. The Bulghārs adopted Islam in the early fourth/tenth century, and it remained their religion until the demise of their state in the wake of the attacks of the Mongols and their subsequent integration into the Golden Horde.

Bennigsen, E. "Contribution à l'étude du commerce des fourrures russes. La route de la Volga avant l'invasion mongole et le royaume des Bulghars." *Cahiers du Monde russe et soviétique* 19 (1978): 385–99.

Erdal, M. *Die Sprache der wolgabolgarischen Inschriften*. Wiesbaden: Harrassowitz, 1993.

Hakimzjanov, F. S. "New Volga Bulgarian Inscriptions." *Acta Orientalia* 40, no. 1 (1986): 173–77.

Hrbek, I. "Bulghār." In *Encyclopaedia of Islam*, 2nd ed. Leiden: Brill, 1986, 1:1304–08.

Khalikov, A. H., and J. G. Muhametshin. "Unpublished Volga Bulgarian Inscriptions." *Acta Orientalia* 31, no. 1 (1977): 107–25.

Mako, G. "The Islamization of the Volga Bulghars: A Question Reconsidered." *Archivum Eurasiae Medii Aevi* 18 (2011): 199–223.

Noonan, Thomas S. "Volga Bulghāria's Tenth-Century Trade with Sāmānid Central Asia." *Archivum Eurasiae Medii Aevi* 11 (2000–2001): 140–218.

Smirnov, A. P. *Volzhskie Bulgary*. Moscow: Izdatelstvo Gosudarstvennogo istoricheskogo muzeĭà, 1951.
Vladimirov, G. "Histoire et culture de la Bulgarie de Volga (traits spécifiques)." *Bulgarian Historical Review/Revue Bulgare d'Histoire* 34, nos. 3–4 (2006): 3–24.
Zimonyi, I. *The Origins of the Volga Bulghars*. Szeged: Attila József University, 1990.
———. "Volga Bulghars and Islam." In *Bamberger Zentralasienstudien*, edited by Ingeborg Baldauf and Michael Friederich, 235–40. Berlin: Schwarz, 1994.

The Rūsiyyah/Rūs

The identity of the people called al-Rūsiyyah or al-Rūs in Arabic writings has long been debated, not least with regard to the Slavic state that emerged in the course of the fourth/tenth century. In Ibn Faḍlān's account, the Rūs are traders who set up camp in or near Bulghār territory, and he gives us a unique eyewitness description of their community that has inspired several studies.

Danylenko, A. "The Name 'Rus'': In Search of a New Dimension." *Jahrbücher für Geschichte Osteuropas* 52 (2004): 1–32.
Duczko, W. *Viking Rus: Studies on the Presence of Scandinavians in Eastern Europe*. Leiden: Brill, 2004.
*Franklin, S., and J. Shepard. *The Emergence of Rus, 750–1200*. London and New York: Longman, 1996.
Golden, P. B. "The Question of the Rus' Qağanate." *Archivum Eurasiae Medii Aevi* 2 (1982): 77–97 [reprinted as Article V in his *Nomads and Their Neighbours*].
———. "Rūs." In *Encyclopaedia of Islam*, 2nd ed. Leiden: Brill, 1995, 8:618–29.
Hraundal, Th. J. *The Rūs in Arabic Sources: Cultural Contacts and Identity*. PhD diss., University of Bergen, 2013.
Montgomery, J. E. "Ibn Faḍlān and the Rūsiyyah." *Journal of Arabic and Islamic Studies* 3 (2000): 1–25.

*———. "Arabic Sources on the Vikings." In *The Viking World*, edited by S. Brink and N. Price, 550–61. Oxford and New York: Routledge, 2008.

———. "Vikings and Rus in Arabic Sources." In *Living Islamic History*, edited by Y. Suleiman, 151–65. Edinburgh: Edinburgh University Press, 2010.

Noonan, Thomas S. "When Did Rūs/Rus' Merchants First Visit Khazaria and Baghdad?" *Archivum Eurasiae Medii Aevi* 7 (1987–91): 213–19.

A large part of Ibn Faḍlān's description of the Rūs describes an intriguing, if violent, funerary ceremony:

Lewicki, T. "Les rites funéraires païens des Slavs occidentaux et des anciens russes d'après les relations—remontant surtout aux IX-Xe siècles—des voyageurs et des écrivains arabes." *Folia Orientalia* 5 (1963): 1–74.

Price, N. "Passing into Poetry: Viking Age Mortuary Drama and the Origins of Norse Mythology." *Medieval Archaeology* 54 (2010): 123–57.

Sass, T., and M. L. Warmind. "Mission Saqaliba." *Chaos* 11 (1989): 31–49.

Schjødt, J. P. "Ibn Faḍlān's Account of a Rus Funeral: To What Degree Does It Reflect Nordic Myths?" In *Reflections on Old Norse Myths*, edited by P. Hermann, J. P. Schjødt, and R. T. Kristensen, 133–48. Turnhout: Brepols, 2007.

*Taylor, T. *The Buried Soul: How Humans Invented Death*. London: Beacon Press, 2002 [the relevant sections are pp. 86–112 and 170–93].

The Khazars

The empire of the Khazar *khāqān* emerged in the early first/seventh century and remained the most important entity on the Eurasian steppe for many centuries. Occasional allies of Byzantium, the Khazars fought off Muslim advances via the Caucasus in the first/seventh and second/eighth centuries, subsequently maintaining a more peaceful relationship with the caliphate, conducted mainly through trade. The Arabic sources state that, at some point, the elite surrounding the house of the *khāqān* converted to Judaism.

Barthold, W., and P. B. Golden. "Khazar." In *Encyclopaedia of Islam*, 2nd ed. Leiden: Brill, 1997, 2:1172–81.
*Brook, Kevin A. *The Jews of Khazaria*. Northvale, NJ: Aronson, 1999.
———. "Khazar-Byzantine Relations." In *The Turks*. Vol. 1, *Early Ages*, edited by Hasan Celâl Güzel, C. Cem Oğuz, and Osman Karatay, 509–14. Ankara: Yeni Türkiye, 2002.
Czeglédy, K. "Khazar Raids in Transcaucasia in AD 762–764." *Acta Orientalia* 11, no. 1 (1960): 75–88.
———. "Notes on Some Problems of the Early Khazar History." In *Trudy Dvadtsat' pyatogo Mezhdunarodnogo Kongressa Vostokovedov, Moskva 1960*, edited by B. G. Gafurov, vol. 3, 336–38. Moscow: Izdatelstvo Vostochnoi Literatury, 1963.
*Dunlop, D. M. *The History of the Jewish Khazars*. Princeton: Princeton University Press, 1954.
Flyorova, V. E. *Obrazy i siuzhety mifologii Khazarii [The Images and Topics of Khazarian Mythology]*. Jerusalem: Gesharim and Moscow: Mosty Kul'tury: Evreĭskiĭ universitet v Moskve, 2001.
Golden, Peter B. *Khazar Studies: An Historico-Philological Inquiry into the Origins of the Khazars*. Budapest: Akadémiai Kiadó, 1980.
———. "Khazaria and Judaism." *Archivum Eurasiae Medii Aevi* 3 (1983): 127–56 [reprinted as Article III in his *Nomads and their Neighbours*].
———. "Some Notes on the Comitatus in Medieval Eurasia with Special Reference to the Khazars." *Histoire Russe* 28, no. 1 (2001), 153–70.
———. *Nomads and Their Neighbours in the Russian Steppe: Turks, Khazars and Qipchaqs*. Aldershot: Variorum, 2003.
———. "Irano-Turcica: The Khazar Sacral Kingship Revisited." *Acta Orientalia* 60, no. 2 (2007): 161–94 [reprinted as Article X in his *Turks and Khazars*].
———. *Turks and Khazars: Origins, Institutions, and Interactions in Pre-Mongol Eurasia*. Aldershot: Variorum, 2010.
Klyashtorny, S. G. "About One Khazar Title in Ibn Faḍlān." *Manuscripta Orientalia* 3, no. 3 (1997): 22–23.
Mako, G. "The Possible Reasons for the Arab-Khazar Wars." *Archivum Eurasiae Medii Aevi* 17 (2010): 45–57.

Mason, R. A. E. "The Religious Beliefs of the Khazars." *Ukrainian Quarterly* 51, no. 4 (1995): 383–415.

Naimushin, B. "Khazarskii kaganat i vostochnaia Evropa: Stolkovenia mezhdu 'kochevnikami stepei' i 'kochevnikami rek'" [The Khazar Kaghanate and Eastern Europe: Collision between the "Nomads of the Steppe" and the "Nomads of the Rivers"]. In *Bâlgari i Xazari: Prez Rannoto Srednovekovie*, edited by Tsvetelin Stepanov, 142–58. Sofia: TANGRA, 2003.

Noonan, T. S. "What Does Historical Numismatics Suggest about the History of Khazaria in the Ninth Century?" *Archivum Eurasiae Medii Aevi* 3 (1983): 265–81.

———. "Why Dirhams First Reached Russia: The Role of Arab-Khazar Relations in the Development of the Earliest Islamic Trade with Eastern Europe." *Archivum Eurasiae Medii Aevi* 4 (1984): 151–282 [reprinted as Article II in his *The Islamic World*].

———. "Khazaria as an Intermediary between Islam and Eastern Europe in the Second Half of the Ninth Century: The Numismatic Perspective." *Archivum Eurasiae Medii Aevi* 5 (1985): 179–204.

———. "Byzantium and the Khazars: A Special Relationship?" In *Byzantine Diplomacy: Papers from the Twenty-Fourth Spring Symposium of Byzantine Studies, Cambridge, March 1990*, edited by J. Shepard and S. Franklin, 109–32. Aldershot: Variorum, 1992.

———. "The Khazar Economy." *Archivum Eurasiae Medii Aevi* 9 (1995–97): 253–318.

———. "The Khazar-Byzantine World of the Crimea in the Early Middle Ages: The Religious Dimension." *Archivum Eurasiae Medii Aevi* 10 (1999): 207–30.

———. "Nomads and Sedentarists in a Multi-Ethnic Empire: The Role of the Khazars in the Khazar Khaganate." *Archivum Eurasiae Medii Aevi* 15 (2006–7): 107–24.

Olsson, J. "Coup d'état, Coronation and Conversion: Some Reflections on the Adoption of Judaism by the Khazar Khaganate." *Journal of the Royal Asiatic Society* 23, no. 4 (2013): 495–526.

Pletneva, S. *Ocherki Khazarskoĭ arkheologii [Essays on Khazar Archaeology]*. Jerusalem: Gesharim and Moscow: Mosty Kul'tury, 1999. [A collection of Pletneva's important contributions to Khazar archaeology, with an afterword in English by Vladimir Petrukhin.]

Polgár, S. "A Contribution to the History of the Khazar Military Organization: The Strengthening of the Camp." *Acta Orientalia* 58, no. 2 (2005): 197–204.

Romashov, S. A. "Istoricheskaya geografia khazarskogo kaganata (V-XIII vv) [The Historical Geography of the Khazar Kaghanate (5th-13th c.)]." *Archivum Eurasiae Medii Aevi* 11 (2000–1): 219–338.

Shapira, D. "Two Names of the First Khazar Jewish Beg." *Archivum Eurasiae Medii Aevi* 10 (1999): 231–41.

Shepard, J. "The Khazars' Formal Adoption of Judaism and Byzantium's Northern Policy." *Oxford Slavonic Papers* 31 (1998): 11–34.

Togan, A. Zeki Velidi. "Völkerschaften des Chazarenreiches im neunten Jahrhundert." In *Texts and Studies on the Historical Geography and Topography of Northern and Eastern Europe*, edited by Fuat Sezgin, with M. Amawi, C. Ehrig-Eggert, and E. Neubauer, vol. 3, 302–38. Frankfurt am Main: Institute for the History of Arabic-Islamic Science at the Johann Wolfgang Goethe University, 1994.

Zadeh, M. S. "Khazars in Islamic Sources." *Amu Darya* 4, no. 6 (2000): 273–96.

Zuckermann, C. "On the Origin of the Khazar Diarchy and the Circumstances of Khazaria's Conversion to Judaism." In *The Turks*. Vol. 1, *Early Ages*, edited by H. Celâl Güzel, C. Cem Oğuz, and O. Karatay, 516–23. Ankara: Yeni Türkiye, 2002.

Index

Index references beginning with "Y" refer to "Yāqūt's Quotations from the Book of Ibn Faḍlān," on pp.41–62. References beginning with the symbol (§) refer to the main text, and are listed by section number, for ease of cross-reference with the hardcover and electronic editions. All other references in the following index refer to page numbers within the book.

About the NYU Abu Dhabi Institute

The Library of Arabic Literature is supported by a grant from the NYU Abu Dhabi Institute, a major hub of intellectual and creative activity and advanced research. The Institute hosts academic conferences, workshops, lectures, film series, performances, and other public programs directed both to audiences within the UAE and to the worldwide academic and research community. It is a center of the scholarly community for Abu Dhabi, bringing together faculty and researchers from institutions of higher learning throughout the region.

NYU Abu Dhabi, through the NYU Abu Dhabi Institute, is a world-class center of cutting-edge research, scholarship, and cultural activity. The Institute creates singular opportunities for leading researchers from across the arts, humanities, social sciences, sciences, engineering, and the professions to carry out creative scholarship and conduct research on issues of major disciplinary, multidisciplinary, and global significance.

About the Translator

James E. Montgomery is Sir Thomas Adams's Professor of Arabic and Fellow of Trinity Hall at the University of Cambridge. He juggles many fascinations. Some of them he has had for many years now though he has probably discarded even more over the years. His current fascinations are: the body of writings attributed to al-Jāḥiẓ (d. 255/868–69); Arabic hunting poetry of the third/ninth century; the music of Björk and the poetry of Simon Armitage; the Library of Arabic Literature. He is lucky to have a wonderful wife, three amazing children, and two brilliant dogs. He is training to deadlift 200 kg and likes to get out of Cambridge and go to Yorkshire as often as possible.

The Library of Arabic Literature

For more details on individual titles, visit www.libraryofarabicliterature.org.

Classical Arabic Literature: A Library of Arabic Literature Anthology
Selected and translated by Geert Jan van Gelder

A Treasury of Virtues: Sayings, Sermons and Teachings of ʿAlī, by al-Qāḍī al-Quḍāʿī with the *One Hundred Proverbs* attributed to al-Jāḥiẓ
Edited and translated by Tahera Qutbuddin

The Epistle on Legal Theory, by al-Shāfiʿī
Edited and translated by Joseph E. Lowry

Leg over Leg, by Aḥmad Fāris al-Shidyāq
Edited and translated by Humphrey Davies

Virtues of the Imām Aḥmad ibn Ḥanbal, by Ibn al-Jawzī
Edited and translated by Michael Cooperson

The Epistle of Forgiveness, by Abū l-ʿAlāʾ al-Maʿarrī
Edited and translated by Geert Jan van Gelder and Gregor Schoeler

The Principles of Sufism, by ʿĀʾishah al-Bāʿūniyyah
Edited and translated by Th. Emil Homerin

The Expeditions: An Early Biography of Muḥammad, by Maʿmar ibn Rāshid
Edited and translated by Sean W. Anthony

Two Arabic Travel Books
Accounts of China and India, by Abū Zayd al-Sīrāfī
Edited and translated by Tim Mackintosh-Smith

Mission to the Volga, by Aḥmad ibn Faḍlān
Edited and translated by James Montgomery

Disagreements of the Jurists: A Manual of Islamic Legal Theory, by al-Qāḍī al-Nuʿmān
Edited and translated by Devin J. Stewart

Consorts of the Caliphs: Women and the Court of Baghdad, by Ibn al-Sāʿī
Edited by Shawkat M. Toorawa and translated by the Editors of the Library of Arabic Literature

What ʿĪsā ibn Hishām Told Us, by Muḥammad al-Muwayliḥī
Edited and translated by Roger Allen

The Life and Times of Abū Tammām, by Abū Bakr Muḥammad ibn Yaḥyā al-Ṣūlī
Edited and translated by Beatrice Gruendler

The Sword of Ambition: Bureaucratic Rivalry in Medieval Egypt, by ʿUthmān ibn Ibrāhīm al-Nābulusī
Edited and translated by Luke Yarbrough

Brains Confounded by the Ode of Abū Shādūf Expounded, by Yūsuf al-Shirbīnī
Edited and translated by Humphrey Davies

Light in the Heavens: Sayings of the Prophet Muḥammad, by al-Qāḍī al-Quḍāʿī
Edited and translated by Tahera Qutbuddin

Risible Rhymes, by Muḥammad ibn Maḥfūẓ al-Sanhūrī
Edited and translated by Humphrey Davies

A Hundred and One Nights
Edited and translated by Bruce Fudge

The Excellence of the Arabs, by Ibn Qutaybah
Edited by James E. Montgomery and Peter Webb
Translated by Sarah Bowen Savant and Peter Webb

Scents and Flavors: A Syrian Cookbook
Edited and translated by Charles Perry

English-only Paperbacks

Leg over Leg: Volumes One and Two, by Aḥmad Fāris al-Shidyāq

Leg over Leg: Volumes Three and Four, by Aḥmad Fāris al-Shidyāq

The Expeditions: An Early Biography of Muḥammad, by Maʿmar ibn Rāshid

The Epistle on Legal Theory: A Translation of al-Shāfiʿī's Risālah, by al-Shāfiʿī

The Epistle of Forgiveness, by Abū l-ʿAlāʾ al-Maʿarrī

The Principles of Sufism, by ʿĀʾishah al-Bāʿūniyyah

A Treasury of Virtues: Sayings, Sermons and Teachings of ʿAlī, by al-Qāḍī al-Quḍāʿī with *The One Hundred Proverbs*, attributed to al-Jāḥiẓ

The Life of Ibn Ḥanbal, by Ibn al-Jawzī

Mission to the Volga, by Ibn Faḍlān

Accounts of China and India, by Abū Zayd al-Sīrāfī